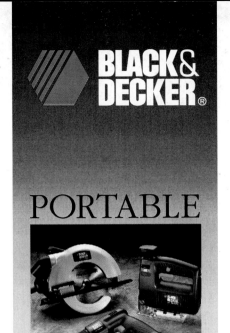

BLACK & DECKER®

PORTABLE WORKSHOP™

Basic Wood Projects W9-CCG-181
with Portable Power Tools

Kitchen Accessories

COWLES
Creative Publishing, Inc.
Minnetonka, Minnesota, USA

Credits

COWLES Creative Publishing, Inc.

President: Iain Macfarlane
Executive V.P.: William B. Jones
Group Director, Book Development: Zoe Graul

Executive Editor: Paul Currie
Associate Creative Director: Tim Himsel
Senior Editor: Bryan Trandem
Managing Editor: Kristen Olson
Lead Project Designer: Richard Steven
Lead Writer: Andrew Sweet
Additional Writers and Editors: Craig Gelderman,
  Karl Larson
Editor & Technical Artist: Jon Simpson
Lead Art Director: David Schelitzche
Art Directors: Eileen Bovard, Gina Seeling
Technical Production Editor: Greg Pluth
Project Designer & Technical Checker: Rob Johnstone
Project Designer: John Gingerich
Technical Art Draftsman: John T. Drigot
Vice President of Photography & Production: Jim Bindas
Copy Editor: Janice Cauley
Builders: Troy Johnson, Rob Johnstone
Production Staff: Laura Hokkanen, Greg Wallace,
  Kay Wethern
Studio Services Manager: Marcia Chambers
Photo Services Coordinator: Cheryl Neisen
Lead Photographer: Rebecca Schmitt
Production Manager: Kim Gerber

Printed on American paper by:
  Inland Press 00 99 98 97 / 5 4 3 2 1

Created by: The Editors of Cowles Creative
Publishing, Inc., in cooperation with Black & Decker.
BLACK&DECKER is a trademark of the Black & Decker
Corporation and is used under license.

Library of Congress
Cataloging-in-Publication Data

Kitchen accessories.
        p. cm.—(Portable workshop)
    At head of title: Black & Decker.
ISBN   0-86573-642-1 (hardcover).

1. Kitchen utensils. 2. Furniture making. 3. Woodwork.
I. Black & Decker Corporation (Towson, Md.)
II. Series.
TT195.5.K58   1997
684.1'04--dc21   97-20287

Contents

Introduction

More and more people, tiring of eating at expensive restaurants or reluctantly bringing another fast-food bucket home for the family, are rediscovering the joy of cooking at home. And like most seasoned chefs, they are finding that a few accessories can make their own kitchen work go much more smoothly and safely.

Kitchen Accessories, the latest volume from The Black & Decker® *Portable Workshop™*, is full of useful projects to enhance the appeal and efficiency of any kitchen. A variety of durable, attractive storage ideas are presented, so you can display your plates, utensils, and pots and pans proudly, yet keep them safely out of the way. Additional projects include a stepstool for hard-to-reach areas and a utility cart for preparing and serving food on the go. Larger projects range from a simple pantry cabinet to a complete kitchen island and a handsome oak dining table.

Every project in *Kitchen Accessories* can be built using only basic hand tools and portable power tools that you probably already own. You don't need a lot of experience, but if you haven't used any of the tools before, it's best to first practice using them on scraps of wood. And you won't spend hours scouring specialty stores for necessary materials. We used only common products sold in most building centers and corner hardware stores to make these items.

For each of the 20 projects in this book, you will find a complete cutting list, a lumber-shopping list, a detailed construction drawing, full-color photographs of major steps, and clear, easy-to-follow directions that guide you through every step of the project.

The Black & Decker® *Portable Workshop™* book series gives weekend do-it-yourselfers the power to build beautiful wood projects without spending a lot of money. Ask your local bookseller for more information on other volumes in this innovative new series.

Organizing Your Worksite

Portable power tools and hand tools offer a level of convenience that is a great advantage over stationary power tools. But using them safely and conveniently requires some basic housekeeping. Whether you are working in a garage, a basement or outdoors, it is important that you establish a flat, dry holding area where you can store tools. Set aside a piece of plywood on sawhorses, or dedicate an area of your workbench for tool storage, and be sure to return tools to that area once you are finished with them. It is also important that all waste, including lumber scraps and sawdust, be disposed of in a timely fashion. Check with your local waste disposal department before throwing away any large scraps of building materials or any finishing-material containers.

Safety Tips
•*Always wear eye and hearing protection when operating power tools and performing any other dangerous activities.*
•*Choose a well-ventilated work area when cutting or shaping wood and when using finishing products.*

Tools & Materials

At the start of each project, you will find a set of symbols that show which power tools are used to complete the project as it is shown (see below). You will also need a set of basic hand tools: a hammer, screwdrivers, tape measure, a level, a combination square, C-clamps, and pipe or bar clamps. You will also find a shopping list of all the construction materials you will need. Miscellaneous materials and hardware are listed with the cutting list that accompanies the construction drawing. When buying lumber, note that the "nominal" size of the lumber is usually larger than the "actual size." For example, a 2 × 4 is actually 1½ × 3½".

Power Tools You Will Use

Circular saw *to make straight cuts. For long cuts and rip-cuts, use a straight-edge guide. Install a carbide-tipped combination blade for most projects.*

Drills: *use a cordless drill for drilling pilot holes and counterbores, and to drive screws; use an electric drill for sanding and grinding tasks.*

Jig saw *for making contoured cuts and internal cuts. Use a combination wood blade for most projects where you will cut pine, cedar or plywood.*

Power sander *to prepare wood for a finish and to smooth out sharp edges. Owning several power sanders (⅓-sheet, ¼-sheet, and belt) is helpful.*

Belt sander *for resurfacing rough wood. Can also be used as a stationary sander when mounted on its side on a flat worksurface.*

Router *to cut decorative edges and roundovers in wood. As you gain more experience, use routers for cutting grooves (like dadoes) to form joints.*

Guide to Building Materials Used in This Book

•Sheet goods:
OAK PLYWOOD: *Oak-veneered plywood commonly sold in ¾" and ¼" thicknesses. Fairly expensive.*
BIRCH PLYWOOD: *A workable, readily available alternative to pine or fir plywood. Has smooth surface excellent for painting or staining; few voids in the edges. Moderately expensive.*
MELAMINE BOARD: *Particleboard with a glossy, polymerized surface that is water-resistant and easy to clean. Inexpensive.*
MDF (MEDIUM-DENSITY FIBERBOARD): *Plywood with a pressed-wood core that is well suited for shaping. Moderately inexpensive.*
PINE PANELS: *Pine boards glued together, cut and sanded. Varying thicknesses, usually ⅝" or ¾".*
TILEBOARD: *Vinyl sheet good resembling ceramic tile. Inexpensive.*

•Dimension lumber:
PINE: *A basic, versatile softwood. "Select" and "#2 or better" are suitable grades. Relatively inexpensive.*
RED OAK: *A common hardwood that stains well and is very durable. Relatively inexpensive.*
CEDAR SIDING: *Beveled lap siding for cladding projects.*

Guide to Fasteners & Adhesives Used in This Book

•Fasteners & hardware:
WOOD SCREWS: *Brass or steel; most projects use screws with a #6 or #8 shank. Can be driven with a power driver.*
NAILS & BRADS: *Finish nails can be set below the wood surface; common (box) nails have wide, flat heads; brads or wire nails are very small, thin fasteners with small heads.*
MISCELLANEOUS HARDWARE: *Door pulls; piano hinges; magnetic door catches; shelf pins; shelf standards; plastic or rubber feet.*

•Adhesives:
MOISTURE-RESISTANT WOOD GLUE: *Any exterior wood glue, such as plastic resin glue.*
TILEBOARD & CONSTRUCTION ADHESIVE: *Sold in cartridges and applied with a caulk gun to bond sheet goods.*
TILE ADHESIVE: *An adhesive specially designed for ceramic tile.*

•Miscellaneous materials:
Wood plugs (for filling screw counterbores); dowels; ceramic or stone floor tile; Plexiglas®; decorative trim moldings; veneer tape; others as required.

Finishing Your Project

Before applying finishing materials, fill nail holes and blemishes with wood putty or filler. Also, fill all voids in the edges of any exposed plywood with wood putty. Insert wood plugs into counterbore holes, then sand until the plug is level with the wood. Sand wood surfaces with medium sandpaper (100- or 120-grit), then finish-sand with fine sandpaper (150- or 180-grit). Wipe off residue, and apply the finish of your choice. Apply two or three thin coats of a hard, protective topcoat, like polyurethane, over painted or stained wood.

Wine & Stemware Cart

This solid oak cart with a lift-off tray allows you to safely transport and serve your wine, and provides an elegant place to display your vintage selections.

CONSTRUCTION MATERIALS

Quantity	Lumber
2	1 × 12" × 6' oak
1	1 × 4" × 8' oak
1	1 × 4" × 6' oak
1	1 × 2" × 4' oak
1	½ × 2¾" × 2' oak*
1	½ × 3¾" × 4' oak*

*Available at woodworking supply stores.

With our versatile oak wine and stemware cart, you can display, move and serve wine and other cordials from one convenient station. This cart can store up to 15 bottles of wine, liquor, soda or mix, and it holds the bottles in the correct downward position to prevent wine corks from drying out.

The upper stemware rack holds more than a dozen long-stemmed wine or champagne glasses, and a removable serving tray with easy-to-grip handles works well for cutting cheese and for serving drinks and snacks. Beneath the tray is a handy storage area for napkins, corkscrews and other utensils. Sturdy swivel casters make this wine rack fully mobile over tile, vinyl or carpeting.

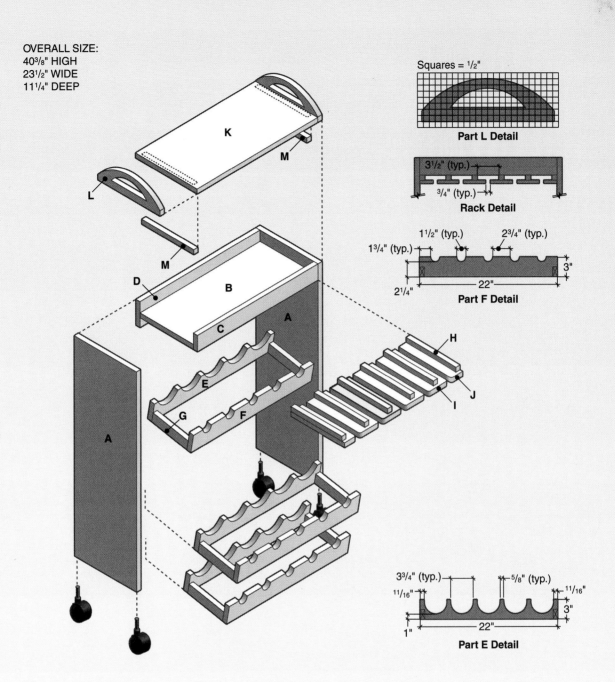

OVERALL SIZE:
40³⁄₈" HIGH
23½" WIDE
11¼" DEEP

Squares = ½"

Part L Detail

3½" (typ.)
¾" (typ.)

Rack Detail

1½" (typ.)   2¾" (typ.)
1¾" (typ.)   3"
2¼"   22"

Part F Detail

K

L

M

M

D

B

C

A

A

E

G

F

H

J

I

3¾" (typ.)   ⁵⁄₈" (typ.)
¹¹⁄₁₆"   ¹¹⁄₁₆"
3"
1"   22"

Part E Detail

Cutting List				
Key	**Part**	**Dimension**	**Pcs.**	**Material**
A	Side	¾ × 11¼ × 34"	2	Oak
B	Top	¾ × 9¾ × 22"	1	Oak
C	Front stretcher	¾ × 2½ × 22"	1	Oak
D	Back stretcher	¾ × 4 × 22"	1	Oak
E	Wine rack, back	¾ × 3 × 22"	3	Oak
F	Wine rack, front	¾ × 3 × 22"	3	Oak
G	Wine rack, cleat	¾ × 1½ × 6½"	6	Oak

Cutting List				
Key	**Part**	**Dimension**	**Pcs.**	**Material**
H	Stemware slat	¾ × ¾ × 9¼"	6	Oak
I	Stemware plate	½ × 3½ × 9¾"	4	Oak
J	End plate	½ × 2⅛ × 9¾"	2	Oak
K	Tray	¾ × 11¼ × 22"	1	Oak
L	Tray handle	¾ × 3½ × 11¼"	2	Oak
M	Tray feet	¾ × ¾ × 9½"	2	Oak

Materials: Wood glue, #6 wood screws (1", 1¼"), casters (4), finishing materials.

Note: Measurements reflect the actual thickness of dimensional lumber.

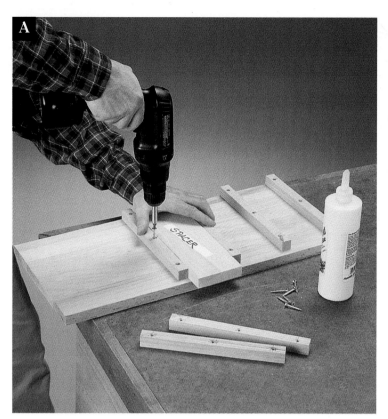

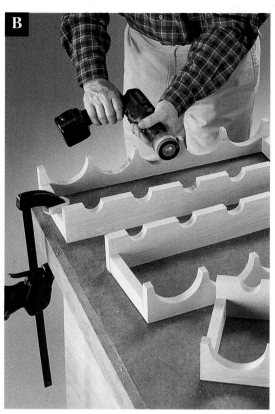

Use a spacer to keep the slats aligned properly, and attach with glue and countersunk screws.

Use a drum sander attached to your portable drill to smooth the curved jig saw cuts on each rack.

Directions: Wine and Stemware Cart

CONSTRUCT THE SIDES AND STEMWARE RACK ASSEMBLY. Start by cutting the cart sides (A), top (B) and back stretcher (D) from 1 × 12 oak. Cut the

> **TIP**
>
> To check for squareness, measure your project from one corner diagonally to its opposite corner. Repeat the procedure for the other two corners. If the two diagonal lines are equal, your construction is square.

front stretcher (C) from 1 × 3 oak, and stemware slats (H) from 1 × 4 oak. Cut the plates (I) and end plates (J) to size from ½"-thick oak. Clamp a belt sander perpendicular to your worksurface, and round over the front corners of the stemware plates, as well as one corner of each end plate. Sand the remaining cut edges smooth with an orbital sander.

Next, position the top facedown, and arrange the slats on the top, flush against the back edge and evenly spaced 3½" apart (use a piece of scrap wood as a spacer). Keep the outer slats flush with the edges of the top. Drill countersunk pilot holes and attach the cleats to the underside of the top piece with glue and 1¼" screws **(photo A).**

CUT AND ASSEMBLE THE WINE RACKS. The wine racks are first assembled as individual units, and are then attached to the sides of the cart.

Cut the wine rack backs (E) and fronts (F) from 1 × 4 oak, and cut the cleats (G) from 1 × 2 oak. Transfer the pattern for the wine rack backs and fronts to each piece (see *Diagram*) and cut them out carefully with a jig saw.

Position the cleats between the fronts and backs of the wine racks, and drill two counterbored pilot holes through the fronts and backs and into the ends of the cleats at each corner. Join the pieces with glue and 1¼" screws, checking to make sure the wine racks are square. Plug the counterbores with glued wood plugs. Clamp each completed rack to

Measure ½" along front and 2½" along back of each side, and connect marks for bottom rack alignment.

Clamp a 4 × 10" spacer between the bottom and middle rack for proper position. Repeat for top rack.

Drive screws through pilot holes in slats to secure top to sides. Counterbore holes through the sides into the top edges, and drive additional screws to secure the top in place.

your worksurface, and sand the curves smooth with a drum sander **(photo B).** Use an orbital sander to smooth the plugs, and any other rough edges.

ATTACH THE WINE RACKS TO THE CART. The racks are installed at a slight angle, to ensure that the wine in each bottle will be in constant contact with the cork. This keeps the corks moist and helps prevent them from cracking and spoiling the wine.

On the inside face of each side piece, measure up ½" from the bottom and make a mark along the front edge. Measure up 2½" from the bottom and make a mark along the back edge. Draw an angled reference line between the marks **(photo C).** With one of the side pieces lying flat on your worksurface, position the first wine rack so the bottom edge is flush against the reference line and the front edge is set back ¾" from the front edge of the side piece. Drill countersunk pilot holes and attach the rack to the side with glue and 1¼" screws.

Attach the middle rack and top rack in the same manner,

using a 4 × 10" spacer to position them correctly **(photo D).**

Using bar clamps, position the opposite side piece, and arrange the stretchers in place between the sides. Check to make sure the unattached cleats are at the proper position and that the stretchers are flush with the top edges of the cabinet. Drill counterbored pilot holes, then use glue and 1¼" screws to anchor the stretchers and remaining cleats. Check frequently during assembly to make sure the cabinet is square.

ATTACH THE TOP ASSEMBLY. Lay the cart on its side, and clamp the top between the side pieces. The bottom face of the top should be flush with the bottom edge of the front stretcher. Drill three evenly spaced horizontal pilot holes through the outer slats into the sides, then use glue and screws to fasten the top to the sides from inside the cart **(photo E).** Drill three evenly spaced counterbored pilot holes through the stretchers into the edges of the top, and secure with glue and 1¼" screws.

To complete the stemware rack, position the cabinet upside down. Center the stemware plates over the slats, with the square end flush against the back stretcher, then drill three evenly spaced counterbored pilot holes along the center of each plate. Attach the plates to the slats with glue and 1"

For consistent placement of the stemware racks, use a ¾" spacer to position the bottom plates on the slats.

TIP

Jig saw blades cut on the upward stroke, so the top side of the workpiece may tear. To protect the finished or exposed side of a project, cut with this side facedown. This way, if the blade tears, it will remain hidden on the unexposed side. Remember to use a faster blade speed if you are cutting with a coarse-tooth blade. When cutting curves, a narrow blade is recommended. Move the saw slowly to avoid bending the blade. Some jig saws have a scrolling knob that allows the blade to be turned without turning the saw.

screws **(photo F).** Attach the end plates to the outside slats with glue and 1" nails driven through counterbored pilot holes.

While the cart is still upside down, drill holes into the bottom edges of the cart sides, and test-fit the casters **(photo G).**

MAKE THE TRAY. The wine cart tray is simply a flat oak board with handles attached to the sides and narrow feet attached below.

While the cart is upside down, drill the bottom edges of the sides for casters.

Drill a pilot hole and then cut the inside handle profile with a jig saw. Use scrap wood to support the workpiece and prevent tearouts.

Cut the tray bottom (K) from 1 × 12 oak, and cut the tray handle blanks (L) from 1 × 4 oak. Also cut the ¾ × ¾" feet (M). Mark the pattern for the handles on the blank (see *Diagram*). Drill a starter hole on the inside portion of the handle, then use a jig saw to cut along the pattern lines **(photo H).**

Position the tray between the handles, then drill three evenly spaced counterbored pilot holes through the edge of each handle. Attach the handles to the tray with glue and 1¼" screws.

Position the tray feet ⅛" in from the sides of the tray bottom and ⅞" from the front and back. Drill counterbored pilot holes, then attach the feet with glue and 1" screws.

APPLY THE FINISHING TOUCHES. Glue ⅜" oak plugs into each counterbore, and sand the plugs flush. Sand the entire cart to 150-grit smoothness, and finish with your choice of stain (we used a rustic oak), and polyurethane topcoat. NOTE: If you will be using the tray as a cutting board, make sure to use a nontoxic finish. When the finish is dry, install the casters on the bottom of the cart.

TIPS

Brushing on a thin coat of sanding sealer before you apply wood stain will help the wood absorb stain more evenly and can eliminate blotchy finishes. Sanding sealer is a clear product, usually applied with a brush. Check the backs of the product labels on all the finishing products you plan to apply to make sure they are compatible.

Plate Drying Rack

This compact plate drying rack is handsome enough to double as a dinnerware display case.

CONSTRUCTION MATERIALS

Quantity	Lumber
1	1 × 2" × 4' oak
1	1 × 6" × 2' oak
1	1 × 10" × 3' oak
3	¾ × ¾" × 2' oak stop molding
7	⅜"-dia. × 3' oak dowels

The holding capacity and clean vertical lines of this plate drying rack could easily make it a beloved fixture in your kitchen. The efficient open design lets air circulate to dry mugs, bowls and plates more efficiently than most in-the-sink types of racks. The rack is handsome enough to double as a display rack to showcase your dinnerware. Even though it has a small 9¼ × 21½" footprint, the rack lets you dry or store up to 20 full-size dinner plates plus cups or glasses. The tall dowels in the back of the rack are removable so you can rearrange them to accommodate large or unusually shaped dishes.

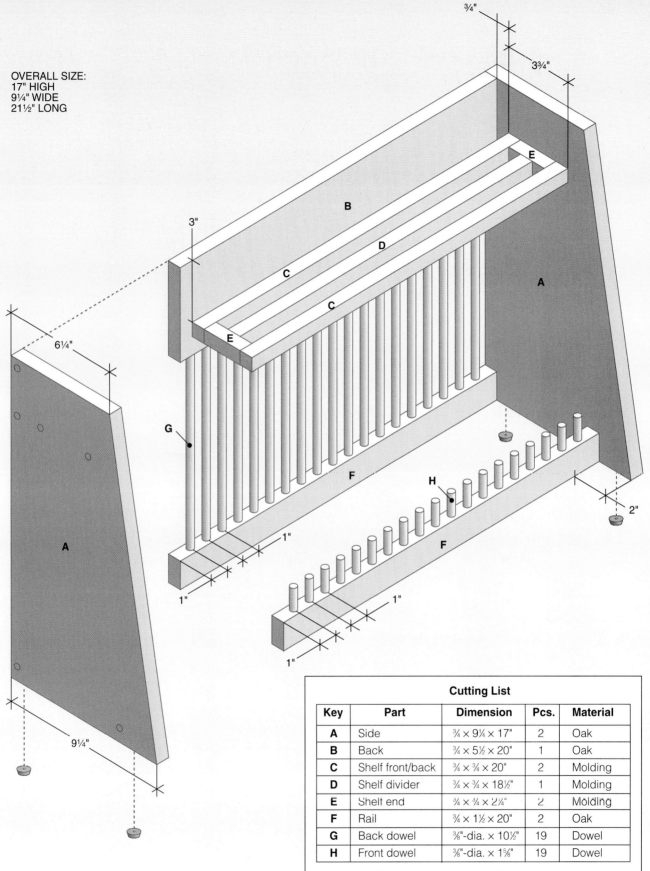

OVERALL SIZE:
17" HIGH
9¼" WIDE
21½" LONG

¾"

3¾"

3"

B

C

D

C

E

E

A

A

6¼"

G

F

H

F

2"

1"

1"

1"

1"

A

9¼"

Cutting List

Key	Part	Dimension	Pcs.	Material
A	Side	¾ × 9¼ × 17"	2	Oak
B	Back	¾ × 5½ × 20"	1	Oak
C	Shelf front/back	¾ × ¾ × 20"	2	Molding
D	Shelf divider	¾ × ¾ × 18½"	1	Molding
E	Shelf end	¾ × ¾ × 2¼"	2	Molding
F	Rail	¾ × 1½ × 20"	2	Oak
G	Back dowel	⅜"-dia. × 10½"	19	Dowel
H	Front dowel	⅜"-dia. × 1⅝"	19	Dowel

Materials: Waterproof glue, #8 × 1⅝" screws, 4d finish nails,
⅜"-dia. flat oak plugs, rubber feet (4), finishing materials.

Note: Measurements reflect the actual thickness of
dimensional lumber.

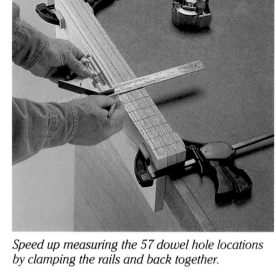

Lay out the sides (A) so they are 9¼" long at the bottom and 6¼" wide at the top.

Speed up measuring the 57 dowel hole locations by clamping the rails and back together.

Directions: Plate Drying Rack

CUT THE SIDES. The sides have a slight backward slant that gives you easier access to the dishes. This slant requires cutting a diagonal line from the top to the bottom. First, lay out and mark the sides (A) so they are 9¼" long at the bottom and 6¼" wide at the top. Connect these marks, and cut along the diagonal line with a circular saw **(photo A).**

CUT AND DRILL BACK AND RAILS. Cut the back (B) and rails (F) to length, and clamp them together. Measure and mark the dowel holes (see *Diagram*) on the edge of each part **(photo B).** Drill the ¼"-deep dowel holes in the two rails, then reset the depth of your drill to ½" and drill the deeper dowel holes in the back.

ASSEMBLE SIDES, BACK AND RAILS. Drill ⅜"-dia. counterbored pilot holes through the sides where the back and back rail will be attached. Apply waterproof glue, and attach the pieces with wood screws.

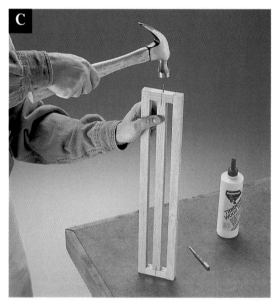

Glue and nail divider in place.

BUILD THE SHELF. Cut the shelf front/back pieces (C), divider (D) and ends (E) to length.

TIP

To make installing the longer 10½" back dowels easier, drill the dowel holes in the back a full ½" deep. When assembling, slide the dowels up into the ½" holes in the back piece and let them drop down into the ¼" holes in the back rail. This lets you easily remove specific dowels to accommodate larger dishes or bowls. Dowel sizes tend to vary so test your dowel sizes by drilling a hole in scrap wood first, using a brad-point bit slightly larger than the ⅜" dowel.

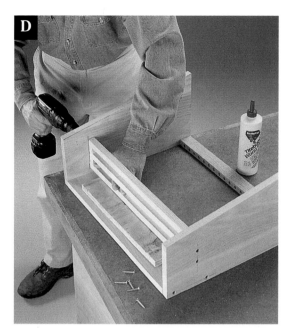

Use a ¾" spacer to position shelf from back while you drill counterbored pilot holes.

Insert dowels into the holes under the back first, then drop them down into the holes in the rail.

Position the shelf front, back and ends together, and drill pilot holes for 4d finish nails. Apply glue, and nail the pieces together. Glue and nail the divider in place **(photo C).** Next, carefully drill counterbored pilot holes through the sides where the shelf attaches. To properly position the shelf, lay the entire unit on its back. Position the shelf 3" down from the top of the rack, using a ¾"- thick piece of scrap material as a spacer between the shelf and the back. Drill the counterbored pilot holes **(photo D).** (Be sure to drill the pilot holes into the long shelf pieces and not through the dividers.) Apply glue, and secure the shelf with wood screws.

CUT AND INSERT DOWELS. Cut the back dowels (G) to length. Position these longer dowels by inserting them up the holes in the back, then dropping them down into the back rail **(photo E).** To complete the front rail (F), cut the front dowels (H) to length. Sand the edges of one end of each dowel. Using waterproof glue, secure the unsanded ends of the front dowels into the front rail holes.

ATTACH THE FRONT RAIL. Position the front rail 2" back from the front edge of the rack, and drill counterbored pilot holes through the sides. Apply waterproof glue, and screw the front rail in place **(photo F).**

APPLY FINISHING TOUCHES. Fill all counterbored screw holes

with oak plugs. Sand smooth the entire rack and all dowels with 150-grit sandpaper. Apply a water-based polyurethane finish, and attach rubber feet to the bottom of the rack.

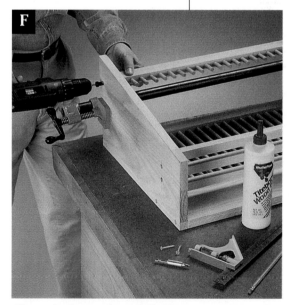

Clamp the front rail, predrill sides, counterbore, glue and screw in place.

TIP

If you plan on consistently using dishes of unusual size, you may choose to change the location of the front rail. The location specified will work well for plates as small as 7" and as large as 11".

Spice Holder

A light, open design keeps all your spices in plain sight and within easy reach.

PROJECT
POWER TOOLS

CONSTRUCTION MATERIALS

Quantity	Lumber
1	1 × 6" × 8' pine
1	1 × 10" × 8' pine

So often, spices for your favorite dishes are hidden away in the back corners of kitchen cabinets—used, and then stuffed behind other cooking supplies without a moment's thought. Until, that is, the next time you are fumbling in a dark cabinet for the oregano while a recipe burns on the stove. Experienced chefs always have a spice holder at arm's length. Ours has four shelves, with space for a variety of ingredients. You can take an instant inventory of your supplies and have favorite herbs handy for sudden culinary inspirations.

The series of arcs cut into the spice holder form a gentle wave that gives the pine construction a soft, flowing appeal, and a small scallop in the back echoes this pattern. The fronts of each shelf are rounded, so you can reach for spices without worrying about sharp edges. Though it's designed to rest on a countertop, this spice holder can also be fitted with an additional shelf and mounted on the wall.

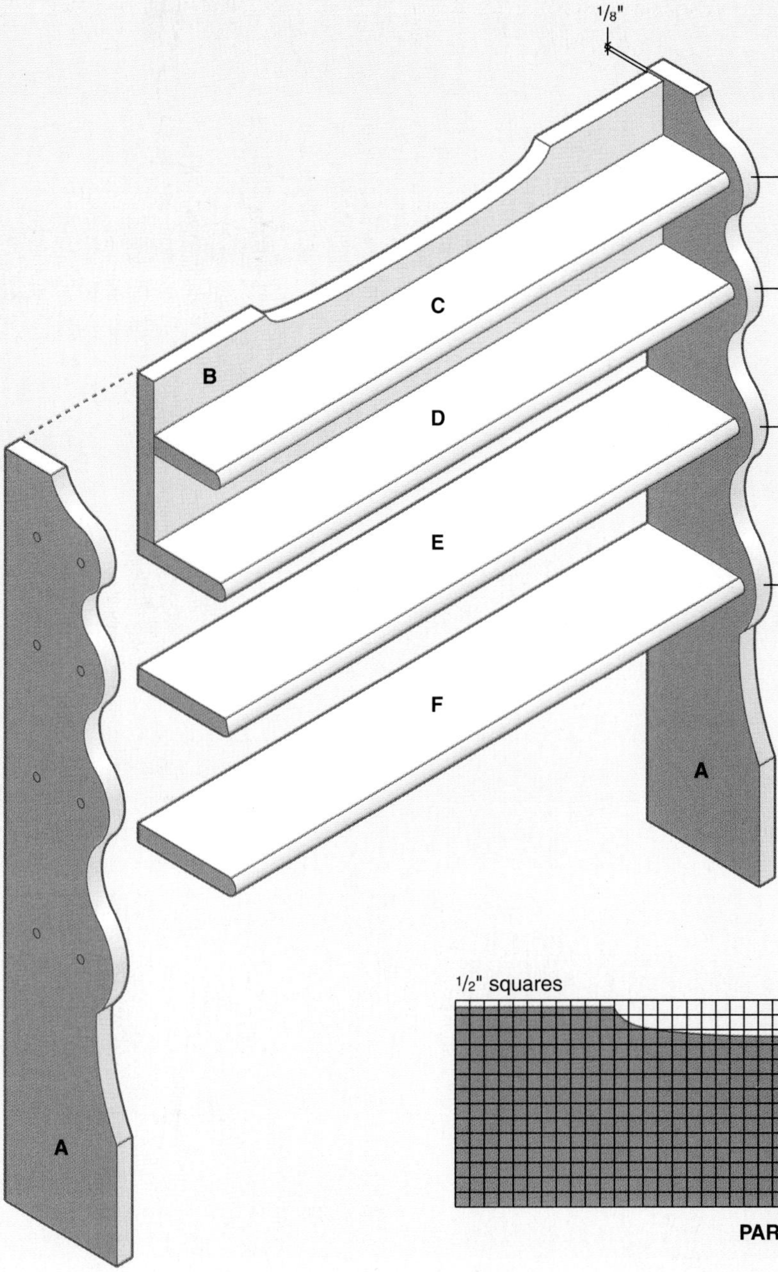

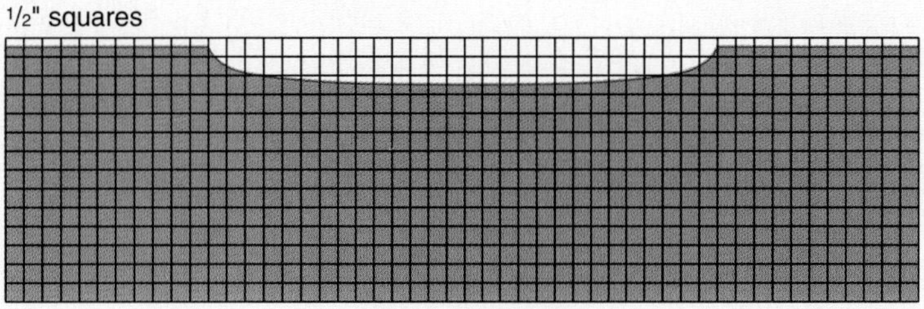

1/8"

OVERALL SIZE:
31¼" HIGH
26½" WIDE
5½" DEEP

1½" radius

1¾" radius

2" radius

2¼" radius

½" squares

PART B DETAIL

Cutting List				
Key	**Part**	**Dimension**	**Pcs.**	**Material**
A	Side	¾ × 5½ × 31¼"	2	Pine
B	Back	¾ × 6¾ × 25"	1	Pine
C	Shelf	¾ × 3¼ × 25"	1	Pine
D	Shelf	¾ × 4¼ × 25"	1	Pine
E	Shelf	¾ × 4½ × 25"	1	Pine
F	Shelf	¾ × 4¾ × 25"	1	Pine

Materials: Wood glue, #8 screws (1⅝"), ⅜" birch plugs, finishing materials.

Note: Measurements reflect the actual thickness of dimensional lumber.

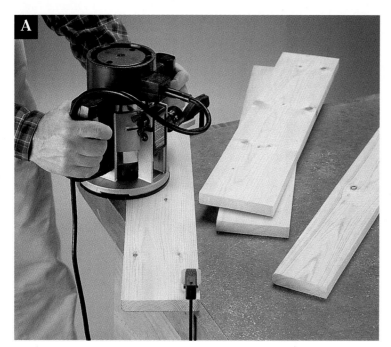

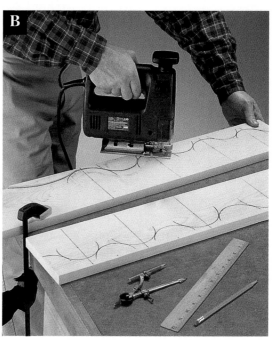

Clamp each shelf to your worksurface for smooth, even router cuts. Flip the shelves to complete each roundover.

Make the side curves with a jig saw. Use clamps to keep parts steady while cutting.

Directions: Spice Holder

MAKE THE SHELVES. The shelves all differ in depth and are cut from dimension lumber. Measure and rip shelves C, D, and E from 1 × 10 pine, and shelf F from 1 × 6 pine, using your circular saw. Clamp each shelf to your worksurface, and round over the front edges of each shelf using a router with a ⅜" roundover bit and bearing guide **(photo A).** Sand all edges smooth.

MAKE THE SIDES. A series of arcs and reference lines indicate cutting lines and shelf positions. Cut the sides (A) to size from 1 × 6 pine, and sand all cuts smooth. Draw reference lines across the sides for the curves and shelves, starting from the bottom of each side, at points 12", 18½", 24", and 28½" along a long edge. The

arcs you draw from the template (see *Detail,* page 19) will be centered on these lines. Transfer the template arcs to each side, and blend all of the arcs together with graceful curves. Clamp each side to your worksurface, and use a jig saw to cut along the arcs **(photo B).**

MAKE THE BACK ASSEMBLY. The back is shaped, then attached to two shelves, providing a framework for the spice rack. Cut the back (B) to size from 1 × 10 stock. Draw a curve 1" deep and 14" long, centered

A drum sander makes sanding curves quick and easy.

TIPS

If you do not own a router, you can complete the roundovers on the front edges of each shelf by planing down the edges with a block plane. You will probably find that planing goes more smoothly, if you plane so the wood grain runs "uphill" ahead of the plane. Don't try to remove too much wood at one time; smooth, easy strokes will achieve the best results. Use an orbital sander to smooth the plane cuts and achieve the proper roundover.

Attach the top shelf to the back assembly from behind with glue and countersunk screws.

Be sure to counterbore all the pilot holes on the sides before driving screws.

on one long edge of the back (see *Diagram,* page 17), and cut with a jig saw. Attach a 1"-dia. drum sander to your drill, and sand the curves of each piece smooth **(photo C).**

Clamp the bottom edge of the back against shelf D, keeping the back flush with the square edge of the shelf. Attach with glue and countersunk 1⅝" screws driven through the bottom of the shelf and into the edge of the back.

When dry, align the top shelf C on the back so the top edge is 2¼" down from the top edge of the back. Glue and clamp in place, and secure with countersunk screws driven through the back and into the shelf **(photo D).**

ATTACH THE REMAINING PARTS. Place the back assembly and remaining shelves in position between the sides. Center the shelves on the reference

lines and keep the back edges flush. Use pipe clamps to hold the spice rack together, and counterbore ⅜" pilot holes through the sides and into the ends of each shelf. Keep the counterbores lined up horizontally for an even look. Remove the clamps, apply glue, and then reclamp, continually checking to make sure the assembly is square. Secure the shelves with 1⅝" screws driven through the counterbored pilot holes **(photo E).**

APPLY FINISHING TOUCHES. Insert glued birch button plugs into each counterbored hole and let dry. Finish-sand the entire project, and apply a light oil or stain, and a polyurethane topcoat.

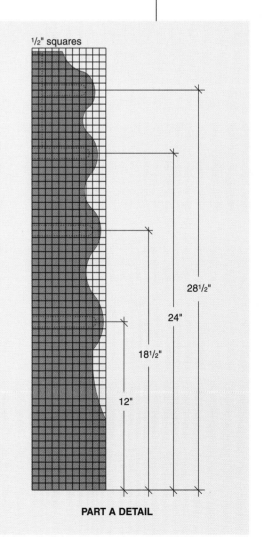

½" squares

28½"

24"

18½"

12"

PART A DETAIL

Vegetable Bin

Whether your vegetables come from the garden or the grocer, our oak bin keeps them organized and out of the way.

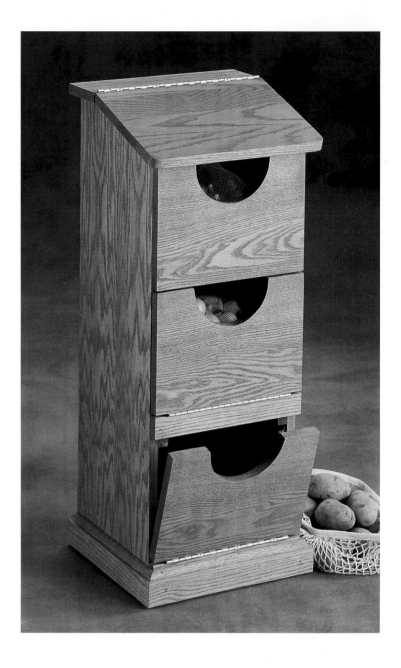

N ot all foods require immediate refrigeration. Onions, potatoes, garlic, shallots and avocados are just some of the foods that don't need to take up precious refrigerator space. But when countertop real estate is also at a premium, veggies often clutter up needed table space or remain in paper bags. Our vegetable bin provides a beautiful, spacious alternative for storing fresh vegetables and fruits. Three separate sections, with hinged bin faces on the sides and top, keep vegetables apart and in place, and make access easy. The sturdy oak construction also provides protection for more fragile items, so your prize tomatoes can stay safely in the shade. The bin's compact vertical design doesn't take up acres of space (just over a square foot), and the rich oak finish trim guarantees a handsome addition to any country (or city) kitchen.

CONSTRUCTION MATERIALS

Quantity	Lumber
1	¾" × 4 × 4' oak plywood
1	¾ × 1½" × 4' oak
1	¾ × 11¼" × 6' oak
1	½ × ½" × 4' quarter-round molding

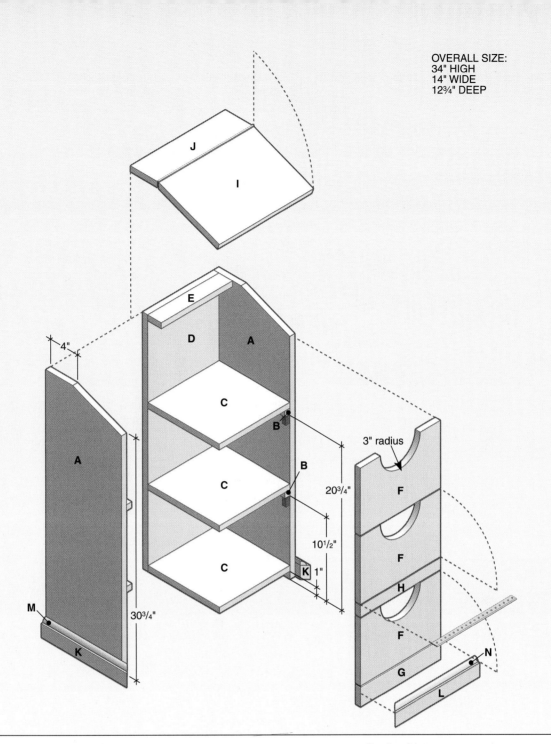

OVERALL SIZE:
34" HIGH
14" WIDE
12¾" DEEP

4"

3" radius

20¾"

10½"

1"

30¾"

Cutting List

Key	Part	Dimension	Pcs.	Material
A	Side panel	¾ × 11¼ × 33¼"	2	Plywood
B	Shelf cleat	¾ × ¾ × 10½"	4	Oak
C	Shelf	¾ × 10½ × 10½"	3	Plywood
D	Back	¾ × 10½ × 32¼"	1	Plywood
E	Top cleat	¾ × 2 × 10½"	1	Plywood
F	Bin face	¾ × 8½ × 12"	3	Oak
G	Lower rail	¾ × 2½ × 12"	1	Oak

Cutting List

Key	Part	Dimension	Pcs.	Material
H	Upper rail	¾ × 1½ × 12"	1	Oak
I	Lid	¾ × 9½ × 14"	1	Oak
J	Fixed top	¾ × 4 × 14"	1	Oak
K	Base trim side	¾ × 1½ × 12¾"	2	Oak
L	Base trim front	¾ × 1½ × 13½"	1	Oak
M	Quarter-round side	½ × ½ × 12½"	2	Molding
N	Quarter-round front	½ × ½ × 13"	1	Molding

Materials: Wood glue, oak-veneer edge tape (20'), #6 × 1¼" wood screws, wire brads (1¼", 1½"), 1½" × 36" piano hinge, magnetic door catches (2), chain stops (2), finishing materials.

Note: Measurements reflect the actual thickness of dimensional lumber.

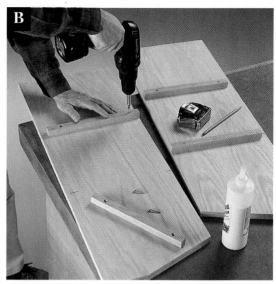

Apply oak-veneer edge tape with a household iron, and trim with a utility knife when cool.

Align cleats on the reference lines, and fasten with glue and screws.

Directions: Vegetable Bin

MAKE THE SIDES. Cut the side panels (A), shelves (C), back (D) and top cleat (E) to size from plywood, and rip the shelf cleats (B) to size from 1 × 12 oak. Sand all edges smooth. Draw a cutline for the front corners on each side panel (see *Diagram*), and cut along the line with a jig saw to shape the side panels. Clamp each side panel in an upright position, and apply oak-veneer edge tape to all edges using a household iron **(photo A).** Let the veneer cool, and trim the edges with a utility knife. Measure and mark cleat and shelf locations across the inner face of each panel, 1", 10½" and 20¾" from the bottom. Drill countersink pilot holes, then use glue and screws to attach the cleats

Use a nail set to recess nail heads flush with the shelves.

to the side panels **(photo B).** The bottom of the cleats should be flush with the marked lines, and the front of the cleats should be flush with the front edges of the side panels.

ATTACH THE SIDES AND BACK. Position the bottom shelf between the side panels so the bottom edge of the shelf rests on the 1" reference line. Keep the front edge flush with the side panels, and fasten with glue and screws. Attach the remaining shelves to the cleats

with glue and 1¼" brads, using a nail set to recess the nail heads **(photo C).** Use glue and screws to attach the back to the shelves. Place the top cleat flush against the top of the assembly, and fasten with screws driven through the back and into the cleat **(photo D).** Drive 1½" brads through each side panel into the ends of the top cleat and the edges of the back piece.

> **TIPS**
>
> *The side panels, shelves, back and top cleat are cut from plywood. The base trim is cut from 1½"-wide oak, while all the remaining parts can be ripped from a single 11¼"-wide board.*

Attach the top cleat from behind with glue and screws, and set in place with two brads at each end.

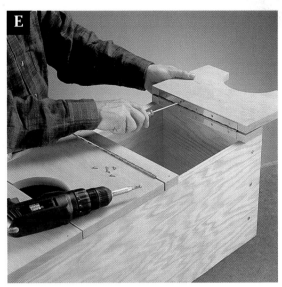

Attach the rails, and then adjust and fasten the bin lids to the hinges.

MAKE THE BIN FACES AND LID. The lower bin faces are hinged for easy access. The upper bin face is permanently fixed, and access is gained through a hinged lid. Rip-cut the bin faces (F) lower rail (G), upper rail (H), lid (I) and fixed top (J) to size from 1 × 12 oak. When cutting the lid, use your circular saw to cut a 10° bevel into the back edge of the lid. On each bin face, mark a centerpoint on one long edge. Draw a 3"-rad. arc centered on each point, and cut each arc out with a jig saw. Sand the cut edges smooth.

Cut the piano hinge into two 11" sections and one 13" section, using a hacksaw. Center the 11" piano hinges on the lower and upper rails. Drill pilot holes and attach the hinges with the enclosed screws. Position the hinged rails on the bin. The lower rail should be flush with the bottom of the bin. The bottom edge of the upper rail should be flush with the middle shelf, 11¼" from the bottom of the bin. Drill pilot holes and attach the rails to the front of

the bin with glue and 1½" brads. Secure the bin faces to the hinges using the enclosed mounting hardware **(photo E).** Lay the upper bin face in position, flush with the bottom of the top shelf. Drill pilot holes and attach the upper bin face with glue and 1½" brads. Center and attach the 13" piano hinge onto the fixed top, drill pilot holes, and fasten with screws. Center the fixed top (hinge up) on top of the assembly, flush with the back edge, then drill pilot holes. Fasten with glue and 1¼" screws driven up through the top cleat into the fixed top. Attach the beveled edge of the lid to the hinge so it folds down correctly over the side panels.

MAKE THE BASE TRIM. Cut base trim sides (K) and base trim front (L) from 1 × 2 oak, and cut the quarter-round sides (M) and quarter-round front (N) to length, mitering the butting ends at 45° angles. Drill pilot holes and attach the base trim pieces with glue and 1¼" brads, and add the

quarter-round pieces above the base trim.

APPLY FINISHING TOUCHES. Fill any exposed nail holes, and finish-sand the entire project, using caution around veneered edges. Be sure to apply a nontoxic finish, such as water-based polyurethane, and let dry. Install magnetic catches in the two lower bins, and fasten stop-chains to support the lids when open **(photo F).**

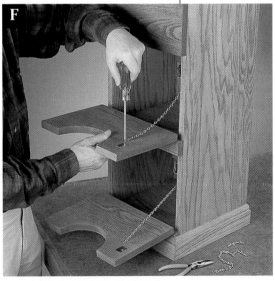

Stop-chains hold bin lids in place when open, and magnetic catches secure the lids when shut.

Pantry Cabinet

This adjustable cabinet provides the versatility needed to organize your pantry.

CONSTRUCTION MATERIALS

Quantity	Lumber
14	1 × 4" × 8' pine
2	¾ × ¾" × 6' pine stop molding

Most pantries are great for storing kitchen supplies or appliances that you don't use every day but still like to have nearby. However, if your pantry itself is poorly organized and inconvenient to use, it winds up as wasted space in your home. To get the most from your pantry, we devised our cabinet for maximum vertical storage capacity. Standing 84" high, the cabinet features three solid shelves for storing heavy goods and two adjustable shelves to fit large or awkward items. You can use this pantry cabinet as a freestanding unit against a wall or as a divider in a larger pantry. The open construction also means you can identify what you have on hand at a glance. Included in the instructions is a simple option for converting an adjustable shelf into a rack that is perfect for stable storage of wine, soda or other bottled liquids.

OVERALL SIZE:
84" HIGH
32" WIDE
12" LONG

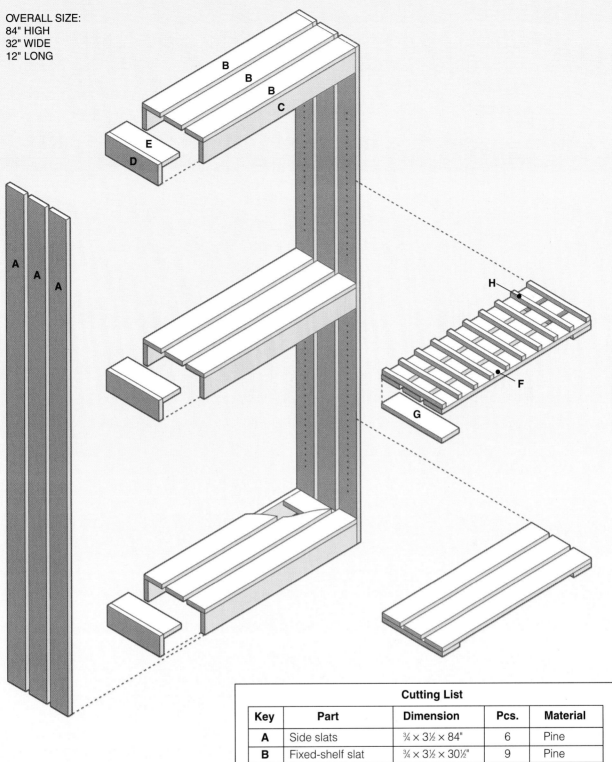

Cutting List

Key	Part	Dimension	Pcs.	Material
A	Side slats	¾ × 3½ × 84"	6	Pine
B	Fixed-shelf slat	¾ × 3½ × 30½"	9	Pine
C	Fixed-shelf face	¾ × 3½ × 30½"	6	Pine
D	Fixed-shelf end	¾ × 3½ × 10½"	6	Pine
E	Fixed-shelf stretcher	¾ × 3½ × 10½"	6	Pine
F	Adjust.-shelf slat	¾ × 3½ × 30⅜"	6	Pine
G	Adjust.-shelf stretcher	¾ × 3½ × 12"	4	Pine
H	Wine-shelf slat	¾ × ¾ × 12"	10	Pine

Materials: Wood glue, wood screws (#6 × 1¼", #8 × 1⅝"), ¼" shelf pins (8), birch plugs (⅜"), finishing materials.

Note: Measurements reflect the actual thickness of dimensional lumber.

Join the shelf faces to the ends by driving 1⅝" screws through counterbored pilot holes.

Apply glue and drive counterbored screws into the shelf faces and shelf ends to connect the stretchers.

Directions:
Pantry Cabinet

MAKE THE FIXED SHELF FRAMES. The fixed shelves comprise the bottom, middle and top of the pantry cabinet. They are essentially box frames that are reinforced internally by stretchers, which in turn help support the three 3½"-wide slats that make up the surface of each shelf. Cut the shelf faces (C), shelf ends (D), and shelf stretchers (E) to size from 1 × 4" pine. Sand the cuts smooth with medium-grit sandpaper. Position the shelf ends between the shelf faces so the corners are flush. Drill ⅜" counterbored pilot holes through the shelf faces into each shelf end. (Keep all counterbores aligned throughout the project to ensure a professional look.) Complete the shelf frame by joining the shelf faces and the shelf ends together with wood glue and 1⅝" wood screws driven through the pilot holes **(photo A).** Repeat for the other two fixed-shelf frames.

ATTACH THE STRETCHERS. Place a stretcher inside the corner of a shelf frame so the stretcher face is flush with the top edges of the frame. Counterbore pilot holes on the shelf faces and ends, and attach the stretcher with glue and 1⅝" screws driven through the pilot holes. Repeat for the other side of the shelf frame and for the other two shelves **(photo B).**

COMPLETE THE FIXED SHELVES. Three slats are fastened to each shelf frame, completing the fixed-shelf units.

Cut the shelf slats (B) to size and sand the edges smooth. Place three slats on your worksurface. Turn one shelf frame over so the stretchers are on the bottom, and place the shelf frame on top of the slats. Move the slats so the corners and

Join the fixed-shelf slats to the stretchers with glue and 1¼"
screws driven through the undersides of the stretchers.

When attaching the side slats, position the outer side slats
so the edge is flush with the edges of the fixed shelves.

edges are flush with the shelf frame. Space the slats ¾" apart and then attach the slats with glue and 1¼" screws countersunk through the bottom of the stretchers into each of the shelf slats **(photo C).** Repeat for the remaining two fixed shelves.

ASSEMBLE THE CABINET. The fixed shelves are connected directly to the side slats to provide stability. The base of the pantry cabinet is wide enough to allow the cabinet to stand alone, so long as the cabinet is square. Make sure all joints are square and the edges are flush during this final assembly.

Cut the side slats (A) to size, and sand to smooth out rough edges. On each side slat, draw a reference line 40" from the bottom end. These lines mark the location of the bottom edge

of the middle fixed shelf. To attach the side slats, align all three shelves on end roughly 40" apart, and lay a side slat over them. Adjust the top and bottom shelves so they are flush with the side slat ends and corners. Adjust the lower edge of the middle shelf so it rests on the reference line. Check that the fixed shelves are correctly aligned and that the corners are square. Counterbore pilot holes through the side slats into the fixed-shelf ends and attach with glue and 1¼" screws.

Position the next side slat flush with the other edge of the fixed shelves, and attach with glue and screws driven through counterbored pilot holes. Center the middle side slat by spacing the slat ¾" between the

outer slats (a scrap of ¾" wood makes a convenient spacer), and attach with glue and screws. With a helper, carefully turn the assembly over so it rests on the attached side slats. Position a side slat over the fixed-shelf ends as before, check to make sure the corners and edges are flush, and attach

TIP

You may find it helpful to clamp workpiece parts during the assembly process. Clamping will hold glued and squared parts securely in place until you permanently fasten them with screws. Large, awkward assemblies are more manageable with the help of a few clamps.

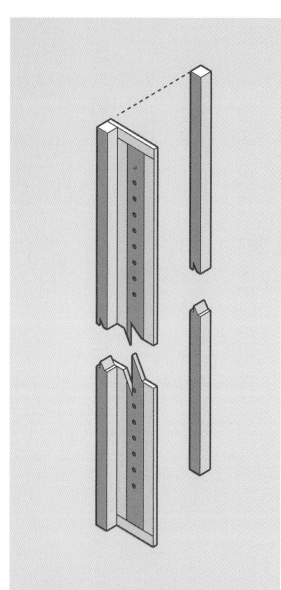

Use a pegboard template for uniform placement of peg holes.

the side slat to the fixed shelves **(photo D).** Attach the remaining side slats to the fixed shelves, checking for square as you go.

DRILLING THE PEG HOLES. The rows of holes on the inner faces of the side slats are used to hold the pegs for adjustable shelving. Using a drilling template ensures that the holes are perfectly aligned, and the shelves are level when installed *(see Tip).*

Begin by wrapping masking tape around the tip of a ¼" drill bit at a depth of ½". This ensures that you do not drill through the side slats. Next, position the drilling template against the inside face of a side slat with the ¾" guide strip resting against the edge of the slat. Drill a row of peg holes along the inner face of the side slat,

using the pegboard holes as a guide. Make sure not to drill beyond the masking tape depth guide attached to your bit.

Next, rotate the template and position it against the other side slat so the other guide strip is resting against the edge of the slat and the opposite face of the template is facing out. Drill another row of holes exactly parallel to the first row. **(photo E).** When finished drilling, sand the slats to remove any roughness.

MAKE THE ADJUSTABLE SHELVES. Our project includes two adjustable shelves, but you can choose to build more. The adjustable shelves are similar in design to the fixed shelves, but without shelf faces or ends.

For each shelf, cut two stretchers (G) and three slats (F), and sand smooth. Lay three slats on your worksurface. Arrange the stretchers over the ends of the slats so the edges and corners are flush, and the slats are spaced ¾" apart. Drill pilot holes through the stretchers into the slats, and fasten with glue and countersunk 1¼" wood screws.

For wine shelving, the design calls for ten wine slats. Cut the slats (H) to size from ¾" pine, using a circular saw and straightedge guide. (Or, you can use pine stop molding.) Sand the cuts smooth. Place the first slat on the adjustable shelf, ⅛" from one end. Keep the ends of the wine slats even with the edges of the shelf slats, and attach with glue and 4d finish nails. Use a 2½"-wide spacer to guide placement for the rest of the slats, and nail in place. Recess all the nail heads on the wine slats with a nail set as you go **(photo F).**

APPLY FINISHING TOUCHES. Using a wood mallet, pound glued ⅜"-dia. birch plugs into all counterbored holes **(photo G).** Carefully sand the plugs flush with a belt sander, and then finish-sand the pantry with fine-grit sandpaper. Wipe the cabinet clean with a rag dipped in mineral spirits. When the wood dries, apply your choice of finish. We brushed a light coat of linseed oil onto the pantry to preserve the natural appearance. If you prefer paint, use a primer and a good-quality enamel. When your finish dries, insert ¼" shelf pins at the desired heights and rest the adjustable shelves on top of the pins.

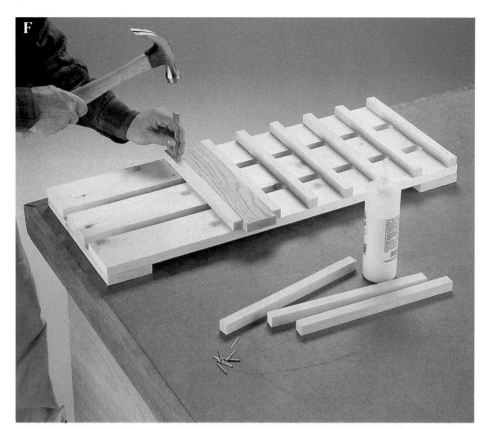

A 2½"-wide spacer helps ensure uniform placement of the wine shelf cleats.

Use a wood mallet to pound glued ⅜" birch plugs in place.

Mug Rack

Your everyday coffee mugs become decorative kitchen items when displayed on this original mug rack.

A mug rack gives you a great way to combine storage and decoration. Just put your mugs in this simple, convenient frame to display them on your kitchen countertop or hang them on a wall. The mugs are always there when you need them, and instead of taking up valuable shelf space, they become decorative kitchen items for all to see. Colorful mug designs look great against the beaded siding board backing on the rack. Paint the project to match your kitchen, or cover it with a clear finish to preserve the natural look of the wood. You can hang your mugs on Shaker pegs, which are easy to install with some glue and a portable drill. Fit the bottom and back of the mug rack with rubber bumpers for increased stability. With a minimum investment of work and expense, you can take a lot of pride in building this mug rack as a decorative home accent.

CONSTRUCTION MATERIALS

Quantity	Lumber
1	1 × 4" × 10' pine
1	1 × 8" × 8' beaded siding board

OVERALL SIZE:
18½" HIGH
3½" WIDE
31½" LONG

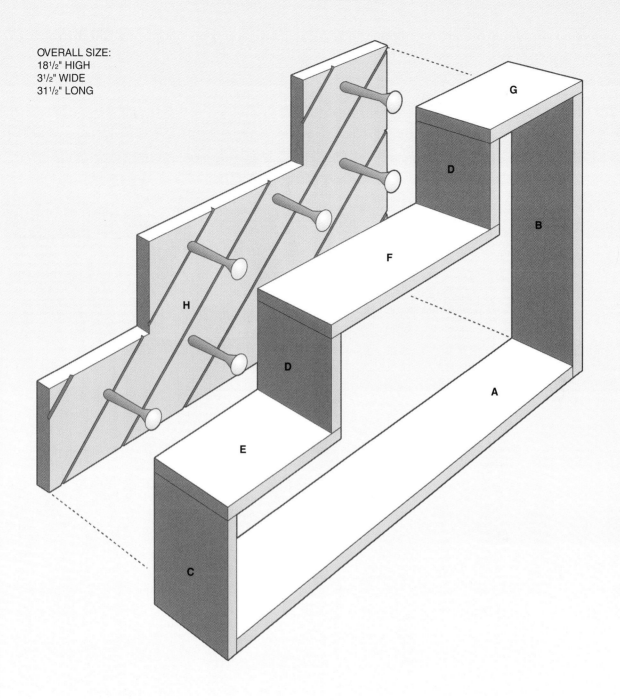

Cutting List				
Key	**Part**	**Dimension**	**Pcs.**	**Material**
A	Frame bottom	¾ × 3½ × 29½"	1	Pine
B	Tall end	¾ × 3½ × 17¾"	1	Pine
C	Short end	¾ × 3½ × 9¾"	1	Pine
D	Divider	¾ × 3½ × 3¼"	2	Pine

Cutting List				
Key	**Part**	**Dimension**	**Pcs.**	**Material**
E	Lower shelf	¾ × 3½ × 7½"	1	Pine
F	Middle shelf	1½ × 3½ × 15"	1	Pine
G	Top shelf	¾ × 3½ × 10½"	1	Pine
H	Backing	18½ × 31½"*	1	Siding

Materials: Wood glue, 4d finish nails, Shaker pegs (8), rubber feet (4), finishing materials.

Note: Measurements reflect the actual thickness of dimensional lumber.

*Cut to fit

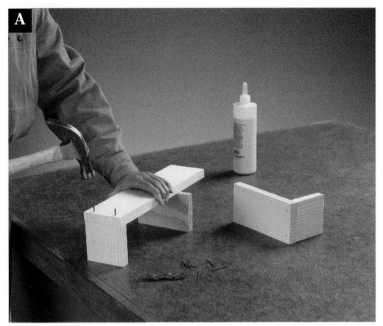

Attach the dividers to the tops of the lower and middle shelves using only glue and finish nails.

Fasten the top shelf to the middle shelf divider.

Directions: Mug Rack

ASSEMBLE THE FRAME. The mug rack frame is assembled completely with glue and finish nails.

Start by cutting the frame bottom (A), tall end (B), short end (C), lower shelf (E), middle shelf (F), top shelf (G) and dividers (D) to size from 1 × 4 pine. Sand out any rough edges with medium (100- or 120-grit) sandpaper, then finish-sand with fine (150- or 180-grit) sandpaper.

Fasten the ends to the bottom with glue and 4d finish nails driven through the ends into the frame bottom edges. Make sure the edges are flush. Next, attach the dividers to the tops of the lower and middle shelves with glue and finish nails **(photo A).** Make sure the end of each shelf is flush with the end of each divider. Use support blocks to help you keep the pieces stationary on the worksurface.

Once the dividers are attached, fasten the middle shelf to the top of the lower shelf divider. Make sure the divider edges and middle shelf edges are flush. Fasten the top shelf to the middle shelf di-vider, once again keeping the edges flush **(photo B).** Finally, use glue and finish nails to fasten the shelves flush with the tall and short ends to complete the mug rack frame.

BUILD & ATTACH THE BACKING. The backing (H) fits into the frame and holds the Shaker pegs. Make the backing from pieces of your favorite beaded siding. Join the pieces together as necessary to create an 18½ × 31½" panel that is treated as a single workpiece.

Cut the backing, and place the mug rack frame on the pieces so their grooves run di-agonally at about a 60° angle. The backing should com-pletely fill the space inside the frame. Trace the cutting lines onto the back panel, following

> **TIP**
>
> *Siding is available in many different patterns, such as tongue-and-groove, shiplap or channel groove. Each pat-tern has a different joint pattern and appearance. These siding styles all cut easily with a circular saw or jig saw, but be careful of kickback, which can cause the material to jump off the table with dangerous force.*

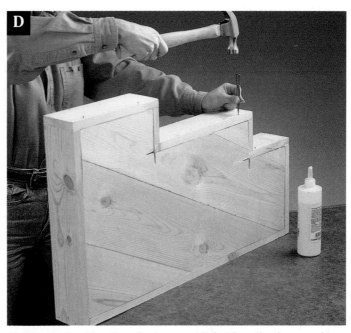

Mark beaded siding positions for realignment.

Fasten the backing into the frame with finish nails, then set the nail holes.

the inside of the frames **(photo C).** Glue the backing pieces together and let them dry. Remove the frame, then use a straightedge or square to re-trace or straighten the lines. Cut the backing to shape with a straightedge guide and a jig saw. Test-fit the backing into the mug rack frame. If needed, trim it to fit the frame. Fasten the backing with 4d finish nails driven through the frame and into the edges of the backing panel **(photo D).** Set and fill all the exposed nail holes. The main section of the project is now complete.

ATTACH THE MUG PEGS. For the final construction steps, you need to attach the mug pegs. Carefully measure and mark the peg locations before drilling.

First, measure and mark a vertical line 4½" from the tall end. Then draw three more ver-tical lines spaced 7¼" apart, marking the peg centerpoints along these lines at 5½", 11" and 16½" from the bottom shelf. Drill ½ × ⅝"-deep holes for the mug pegs at these center-points **(photo E).** Glue and in-sert pegs into the holes. Remove any excess glue.

APPLY THE FINISHING TOUCHES. Make sure all the surfaces are sanded smooth, then paint or finish the mug rack as you see fit. (We used a linseed oil finish on our mug rack.) When the finish has dried, hang the mug rack on the wall, or install rub-ber bumpers on the bottom for stable countertop placement.

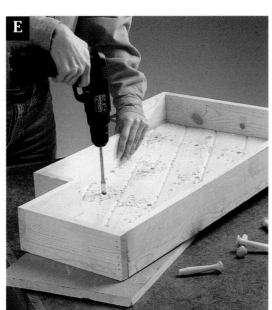

Measure and mark peg loca-tions on the backing, then drill peg holes with a spade bit. Do not drill all the way through the backing.

Bread Box

This easy-to-build bread box creates a safe, crush-proof haven for a loaf of bread or other tasty bakery goods.

The old guessing game "20 Questions" would often start with the query, "Is it bigger than a bread box?" Though bread boxes aren't as common these days, they're still useful items that add a decorative touch to any kitchen, so we decided to revive the old-fashioned bread box. Our classic design emphasizes simplicity, featuring a compact footprint so it easily fits between other appliances, or on a countertop, kitchen table or pantry shelf. The sturdy, oak construction has rounded edges and an angled lid that shows off the rich oak grain and warm color. The solid oak lid is mounted with a 12"-wide piano hinge that helps keep un-wanted visitors out yet provides easy access to your favorite breads or cookies. We stained our bread box and then applied a stenciled label to add a personal touch. Choose a stain or style that matches your kitchen decor, or try adding decorative painting effects like borders, antique letters or rosemaling to add the finishing touch to your own bread box.

CONSTRUCTION MATERIALS

Quantity	Lumber
2	½ × 7¼ × 36" oak
1	¾ × 7¼ × 24" oak

We found ½ × 7¼"-wide oak available in 24", 36" and 48" lengths.

OVERALL SIZE:
8" HIGH
13⅝" WIDE
6" DEEP

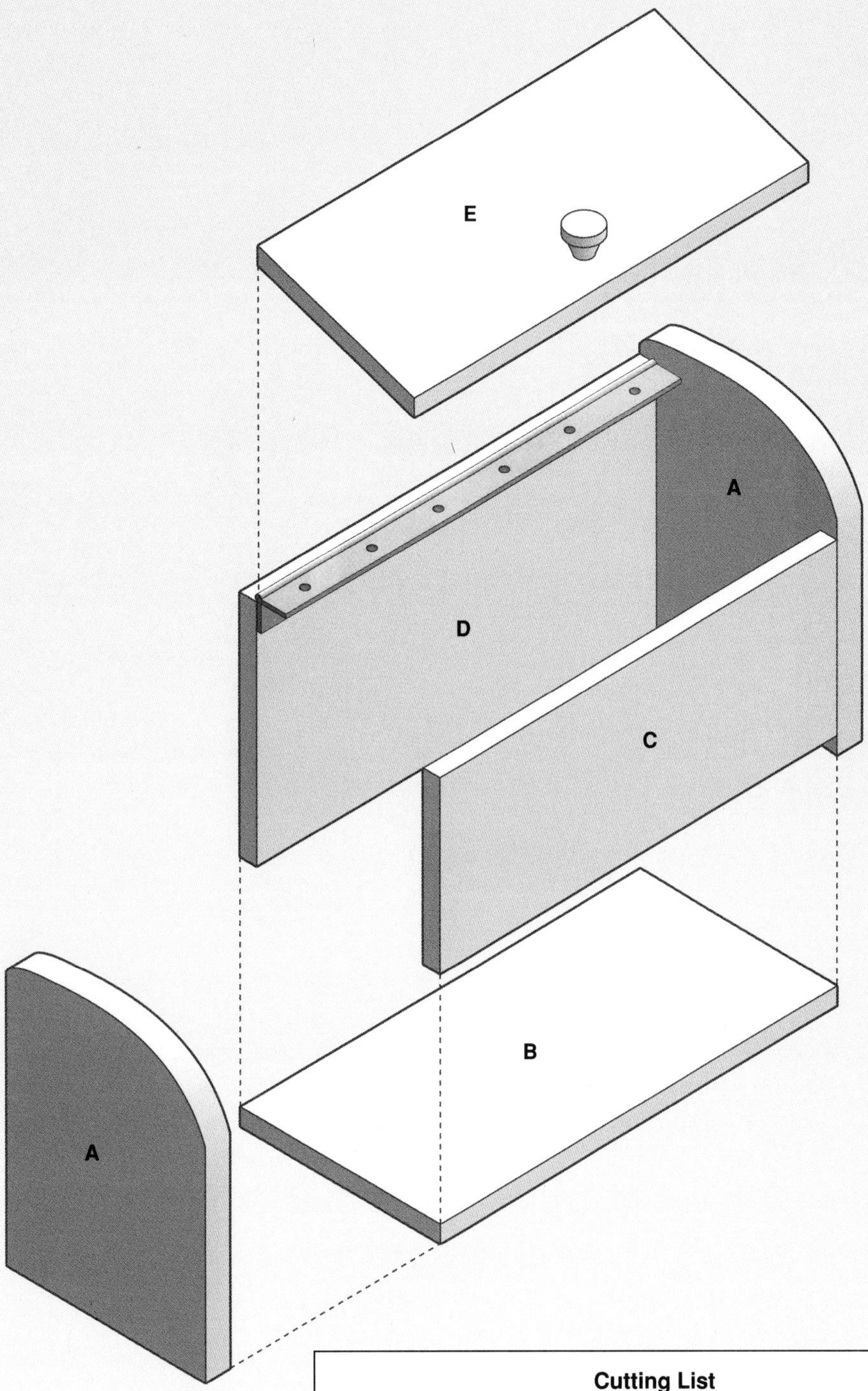

Cutting List

Key	Part	Dimension	Pcs.	Material
A	Side	¾ × 6 × 8"	2	Oak
B	Bottom	½ × 6 × 12⅛"	1	Oak
C	Front	½ × 5 × 12⅛"	1	Oak
D	Back	½ × 6¾ × 12⅛"	1	Oak
E	Lid	½ × 5⅝ × 12"	1	Oak

Materials: Wood glue, 12" piano hinge, porcelain knob (1"-dia. × ¾" length), 4d finish nails, finishing materials.

Note: Measurements reflect the actual thickness of dimensional lumber.

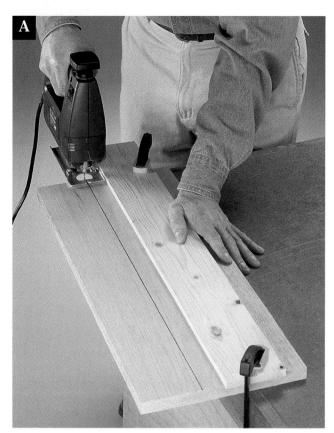

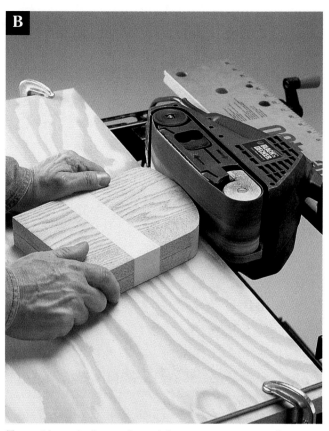

Rip the sides from the same piece of wood using a straight-edge, then cut to length.

Tape sides together and sand the corners to create the profiles on each piece.

Directions: Bread Box

RIP-CUT THE SIDES. The sides are narrower than common lumber width, so it is necessary to rip the lumber lengthwise. Rip the sides (A) to the correct width from ¾" oak lumber. Rip both sides at the same time, using a straightedge to guide your jig saw **(photo A).** Then cut the board to the correct lengths for each side.

PROFILE THE SIDES. The sides are curved to soften the overall profile of the bread box. Transfer the curve outline (see *Diagram,* page 37) onto each side, and cut the rough profile with a jig saw. Tape the sides together, and use a belt sander clamped to your worksurface to sand matching profiles on each side **(photo B).** Take care when sanding. If you remove too much material from the sides, you'll discover after the final assembly that the ends of the lid are exposed.

TIP

When ripping lumber to obtain the correct width, use a straightedge to guide your portable jig saw. Make sure you use a new, sharp blade to minimize rip marks and rough edges. Then belt-sand or block-plane the pieces smooth.

CUT THE REMAINING PIECES. Cut the bottom (B), front (C), back (D) and lid (E) to length from ½" stock. Cut each piece to its appropriate width, and sand all pieces smooth. The bottom, front and back pieces are ⅛" longer than the lid to allow it to swing freely up and down on the 12" piano hinge.

ASSEMBLE THE BREAD BOX. Fasten the back and front to the bottom by drilling 1/16"-dia. pilot holes through the bottom. Glue the front and back pieces to the bottom, clamp in place, and nail with 4d finish nails. Position the sides against the assembly, and drill pilot holes through the sides. Apply glue, clamp and nail.

Attach top by laying unit on back. Position the lid and install piano hinge.

Use a stencil to transfer patterns onto the bread box lid.

ATTACH THE HINGE. Center the hinge on the lid, drill pilot holes, and fasten with hinge screws. Be careful not to drill too far into the ½" wood. Lay the box on its back with the lid in the open position. Open the hinge and fasten the hinge to the back **(photo C).**

APPLY FINISHING TOUCHES. Sand the wood smooth and finish the bread box with your choice of stain. We used a classic walnut stain and a nontoxic water-based polyurethane topcoat. Regardless of the stain you select, it is important to finish the inside as well as the outside of the box and lid. This prevents any warping from moisture and will make clean-

ing the entire box easier. If you decide to add your own graphic element to the lid or to other areas of the box, do so before applying a topcoat. You can personalize your bread box by stenciling words, distressing surfaces to create special antiquing effects, transferring unique designs, rosemaling or using any painting technique of your choice. We created a stencil out of a sheet of plastic and painted a simple graphic on the lid **(photo D).** When the finish has cured, locate and drill a pilot hole for the lid knob, and attach to the lid.

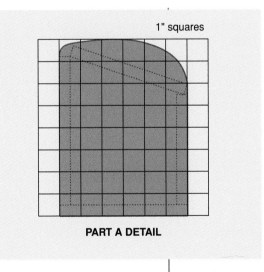

1" squares

PART A DETAIL

Pot Racks

*Turn your kitchen into a space-saving cooking center
with these versatile pot racks.*

CONSTRUCTION MATERIALS

Ladder Rack

Quantity	Lumber
1	1 × 3" × 8' oak
3	1"-dia. × 3' oak dowel

Square Rack

Quantity	Lumber
2	1 × 3" × 8' oak

These inexpensive, easy-to-build oak racks are wonderful pot organizers and great additions to any kitchen, especially if yours suffers from limited cabinet or countertop space. Most busy cooks have one or more overhead racks in their kitchen to keep frequently used cooking items up and out of the way.

Overhead racks also give the proud cook an opportunity to show off copper pans and other gourmet cooking equipment. We've included construction options for a ladder rack with wood dowels, and a larger square rack with lap joints—choose whichever one best suits your kitchen's decor and your personal taste.

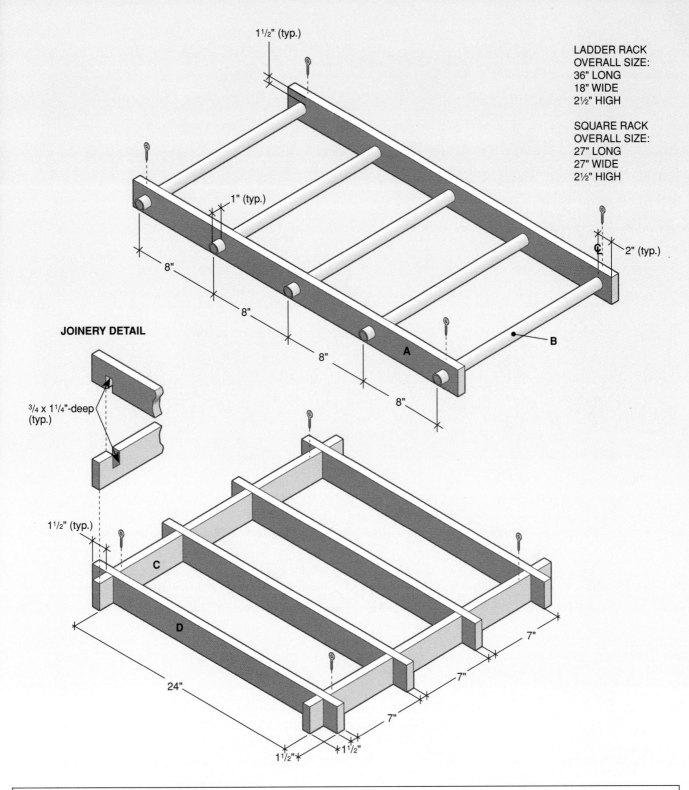

1½" (typ.)

LADDER RACK
OVERALL SIZE:
36" LONG
18" WIDE
2½" HIGH

SQUARE RACK
OVERALL SIZE:
27" LONG
27" WIDE
2½" HIGH

1" (typ.)

2" (typ.)

C

8"

8"

8"

8"

8"

A

B

JOINERY DETAIL

¾ x 1¼"-deep
(typ.)

1½" (typ.)

C

D

24"

7"

7"

7"

1½"

1½"

| Ladder Rack Cutting List |||||
Key	Part	Dimension	Pcs.	Material
A	Stretcher	¾ × 2½ × 36"	2	Oak
B	Dowel	1"-dia. × 18"	5	Dowel

| Square Rack Cutting List |||||
Key	Part	Dimension	Pcs.	Material
C	Rail	¾ × 2½ × 27"	2	Oak
D	Slat	¾ × 2½ × 27"	4	Oak

Materials: Wood glue, 4d finish nails, decorative chain, S-shaped pot hooks, screw eyes (4 for each rack), finishing materials.

Note: Measurements reflect the actual thickness of dimensional lumber.

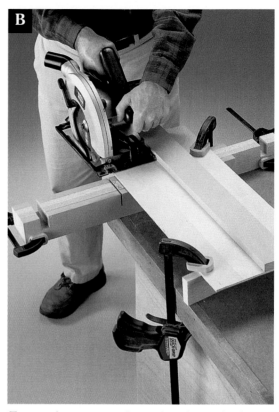

Gang the pieces together and trim the ends with a circular saw and shooting board to remove checks and cracks.

To start the square rack, mark and cut edge lap joints on the rails and slats.

Directions: Square Rack

MAKE A SHOOTING BOARD. A makeshift "shooting board" will help you make clean, accurate cuts across several parts at once. Fasten a 1 × 4 straightedge, approximately 24" long, to a scrap piece of ¼" plywood. Guide your circular saw against one side of the straightedge to trim the plywood parallel. The shooting board holds ganged parts together, and provides a straight, flat guide for more accurate cutting.

CUT THE PARTS. Cut the rails (C) and slats (D) roughly to size. Align the rails and slats, clamp together and trim to length using the shooting board and your circular saw to remove checks and cracks **(photo A).**

NOTCH THE LAP JOINTS. Lay out 4 notches on each rail and 2 notches on each slat for the lap joints. Make notches ¾" wide × 1¼" deep (see *Diagram* for placement). To make uniform cuts, clamp like pieces together—rail with rail and slat with slat—so the joint notches align. Set the depth of the saw blade at exactly 1½" to allow for both the desired depth of cut and the ¼" plywood of the shooting board. Clamp the shooting board in place next to one edge of the notch, and make the cut, keeping your saw flat on the plywood and

tight to the straightedge. Reposition the shooting board, and cut the other side of the notch **(photo B).** Check that the distance between the outside of these defining cuts is ¾". Leave the shooting board in place after the second cut, and, keeping your saw flat on the ¼" plywood, make additional cuts to remove the wood between the first two cuts. Clean any waste from the notch with a sharp ¾" chisel to ensure tight-fitting joints. Repeat this process for all the notches **(photo C).** Take care not to damage the joint edges.

ASSEMBLE THE RACK. Test-fit the rails and slats. Make any adjustments in the lap joints by chiseling, filing or sanding out more stock in the notch. Glue, assemble and finish-nail the square rack together.

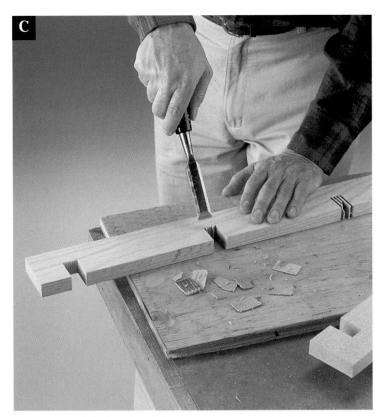

Chisel out debris from lap joints to ensure a good, tight fit.

Place a scrap of plywood under the stretchers to prevent tearouts, and to protect your worksurface.

APPLY FINISHING TOUCHES. Sand the rack smooth and apply a water-based polyurethane finish. Drill pilot holes in the slats, if necessary, and attach pot hooks you've purchased from a hardware store. Thread four screw eyes into the tops of the rails (see *Diagram*). Attach chains to rack, and secure to the ceiling joists with additional screw eyes.

Directions: Ladder Rack

CUT AND DRILL THE STRETCHERS. The stretchers hold the dowels in place and create the outside frame. Trim the stretchers (A) to length with your circular saw and the shooting board, keeping your saw flat on the shooting board and the sole of the saw tight to the guide **(photo A).** Mark the dowel locations on one stretcher (see *Diagram*). Clamp the stretchers together and drill 1" holes using your power drill equipped with a drill guide **(photo D).**

PREPARE THE DOWELS. Double-check that your dowels fit through the holes you're drilling. Cut the dowels (B) to 18" lengths, and, if needed, bevel the ends with a power sander until they fit their respective holes.

ASSEMBLE THE RACK. Secure dowels to the stretchers by drilling $\frac{1}{16}$" pilot holes through the top edges of the stretchers. Drill all the way into the 1" dia. dowel holes. Position the dowels so they extend 1" past the stretchers, glue and fasten in place with 4d finishing nails **(photo E).**

APPLY FINISHING TOUCHES. Sand smooth and apply a water-based polyurethane fin-

Insert the dowels into the holes and secure each with a 4d finish nail.

ish. Attach chains in the same fashion used with the square rack, and secure to ceiling joists with screw eyes.

Recycling Center

Recycling is no longer a chore when this convenient recycling center is a fixture in your kitchen.

CONSTRUCTION MATERIALS

Quantity	Lumber
1	¾" × 4 × 8' birch plywood
1	1¼"-dia. × 36" birch dowel
3	¼ × 3 × 3" Masonite® or scrap wood

Finding adequate storage for recyclables in a kitchen or pantry is a real challenge. Gaping paper bags of discarded aluminum, newspaper, glass and plastic look awful and can be a real nuisance. Our recycling center eliminates the nuisance and makes recycling easy. The recycling center holds up to four bags of recyclables, keeping the materials in one place and out of sight. Arches on the bottom of the cabinet create the four feet and are echoed on the front edges. The two spacious bins pivot forward on a dowel for easy deposit and removal of recyclables, and the top of the cabinet is sturdy enough to serve as a shelf.

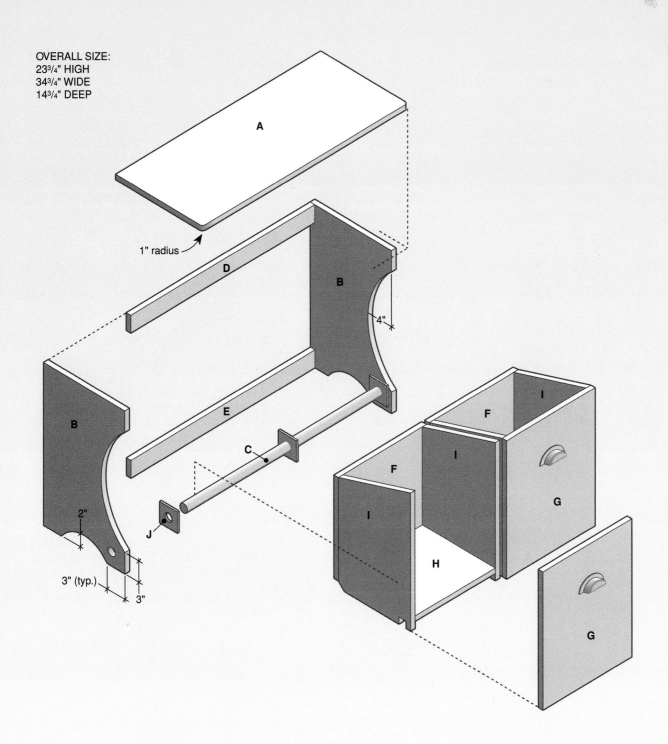

OVERALL SIZE:
23¾" HIGH
34¾" WIDE
14¾" DEEP

1" radius

A

D

B

4"

B

E

C

J

2"

3" (typ.)

3"

I

F

F

I

F

I

G

H

G

Cutting List				
Key	**Part**	**Dimension**	**Pcs.**	**Material**
A	Top	¾ × 14¾ × 34¾"	1	Plywood
B	End	¾ × 13¾ × 23"	2	Plywood
C	Dowel	1¼"-dia. × 34"	1	Birch dowel
D	Top stretcher	¾ × 2½ × 31"	1	Plywood
E	Bottom stretcher	¾ × 2½ × 31"	1	Plywood

Cutting List				
Key	**Part**	**Dimension**	**Pcs.**	**Material**
F	Bin back	¾ × 15 × 16½"	2	Plywood
G	Bin front	¾ × 15 × 19½"	2	Plywood
H	Bin bottom	¾ × 12¼ × 13½"	2	Plywood
I	Bin side	¾ × 12¼ × 19½"	4	Plywood
J	Spacer	¼ × 3 × 3"	3	Masonite

Materials: Wood glue, wood screws (#6 × 1½", #8 × 2", #4 × ⅜"), 4d finish nails, 10" metal chains (2), drawer pulls (2), paste wax, finishing materials.
Note: Measurements reflect the actual thickness of dimensional lumber.

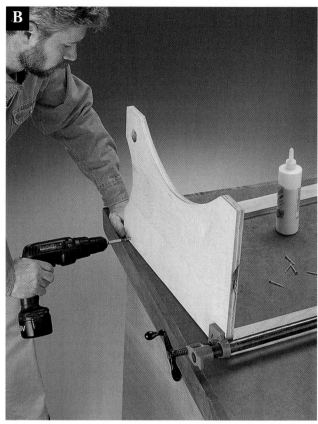

Drill countersunk pilot holes through the bottom edges into the dowel holes.

Glue and drill screws through the frame sides into the stretchers. Use bar clamps to ensure square joints.

Directions: Recycling Center

MAKE THE TOPS AND ENDS. The ends have arches on the bottoms to create the four feet and longer decorative arches on the sides.

Cut the top (A) and ends (B) to size from plywood, and sand the edges smooth with medium-grit sandpaper. To create rounded front corners on the top, use a compass set for 1", and draw the roundovers. Sand the corners down to the curves with a belt sander.

An easy way to draw the arches on the end pieces is to use a thin, flexible piece of metal, plastic or wood as a tracing guide. Along the front edge of each side, make marks 3" in from each corner. Make another mark 4" up from the centerpoint of the front edge. Tack casing nails at these three points. Hook the flexible guide over the center nail, then flex each end to the nails so the strip bows out to create a smooth curve. Trace the arches and remove the casing nails. Draw the curves for the bottom

edges, using the same technique. Along the bottom edges, measure 3" in from the bottom corners and 2" up from the centerpoint of the bottom edge. Tack casing nails at the marks, hook the guide and trace the arches. Make the cuts for the bottom and front arches with a jig saw, and sand smooth with medium-grit sandpaper.

Mark the dowel hole locations on each end piece, 2¼" in and 2" up from the bottom front corner. Use a 1¼" spade bit to drill the dowel holes. Drill countersunk pilot holes for the anchor screws along the bottom edge **(photo A).**

TIP

When checking a cabinet for square, measure diagonally from corner to corner. If the measurements are equal, the cabinet is square. Apply pressure to one side or the other with your hand or clamps to push a cabinet back into square.

Draw reference lines on the top to help center in place when attaching the top to the sides.

Anchor the dowel by driving #8 × 2" wood screws through the predrilled holes into the dowel.

ASSEMBLE THE CABINET FRAME. The top and bottom stretchers form the back of the unit and provide much of its stability.

Cut the dowel (C), the top stretcher (D) and the bottom stretcher (E) to size, and sand smooth. Position the stretchers between the sides so they are flush at the edges and corners, and clamp in place with bar clamps. Drill countersunk pilot holes, then attach the end pieces to the stretchers with glue and 1½" wood screws **(photo B)**.

With the cabinet lying on its back, position the top piece bottom-side-up against the top stretcher, so the edges overlap evenly. Mark the bottom surface of the top piece to indicate where it will rest on the cabinet ends **(photo C)**. Set the cabinet upright and position the top, aligning it with the reference lines. Drill pilot holes, and attach the top to the ends and top stretcher with glue and 1½" screws.

INSERT THE DOWEL. Spacers are placed on the dowel to separate the bins and to give the unit a smooth opening and closing action.

Make the three spacers (J) by cutting 3" squares out of scrap

TIP

Careful planning can prevent valuable wood from being wasted. With the exception of the dowel and the spacers, all the parts for this project can be cut from a 4 × 8' piece of birch plywood (see pattern below):

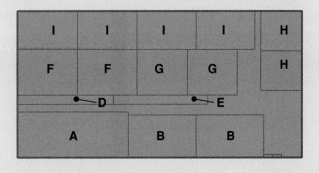

Clamp the bin sides to your worksurface and use a jig saw to cut the notches and bevels.

Position the bin bottom flush with the dowel notch and attach with glue and screws.

¼" material, such as Masonite. Next, locate the centerpoints of the spacers and drill out holes with a 1¼" spade bit to accommodate the dowel. Apply paste wax to the dowel for lubrication. Slide the dowel through one end piece, then through the spacers, and finally through the other end. Position the dowel so it extends out evenly on both sides. Fix the dowel in position by driving 2" wood screws through the pilot holes on the bottom edges of the ends and into the dowel **(photo D).**

MAKE THE BIN SIDES. The bin sides have a notch near the bottom front edge so they can rock safely on the dowel. There are bevels on the top edge and at bottom rear corners to provide clearance.

Cut the bin sides (I) to size, and sand smooth. Use a jig saw to cut a 1¼"-wide, 1"-high notch, located ¾" from the bottom front corner of each bin side (*see Detail,* opposite page). For the short bevel on the bottom, measure and make marks 1" from the bottom rear corner. Draw a cut line between these two marks, and cut off the 1 × 1" corner with a jig saw. For the long bevel on the top edge, measure 2" down from the top back corner and make a mark.

With a straightedge, draw a cut line from the mark to the upper front corner and make the cut with a jig saw **(photo E).** Sand all cuts smooth.

ASSEMBLE THE BINS. The bins are designed to fit underneath the cabinet top. Make sure that all cuts and joints are square so the bins fit properly.

Cut the bin back (F), bin front (G) and bin bottom (H) to size, and sand smooth. Position the sides and front so the edges are flush, then drill coun-

> TIP
>
> *Using a combination square as a marking gauge is much more convenient than making a series of measured points and connecting them with a straightedge. If you need to scribe a line, just set the combination square to your desired dimension, hold pencil and slide square along workpiece, marking as you go.*

tersunk pilot holes and attach the bin front to the bin sides with glue and 1½" screws. Position the bin bottom between the sides so it is recessed 1" and is flush with the top of the dowel notches. Drill countersunk pilot holes, and attach the sides and back to the bottom with glue and 1½" screws **(photo F).** Position the bin back so the top edge is flush with the top of the bin. Drill countersunk pilot holes, and attach the back with glue and 1½" screws.

ATTACH THE CHAIN. To prevent the bins from falling forward when adding or removing recyclables, our design uses chain to attach the bins to the top. The chains can be easily detached from eye hooks when cleaning needs to be done.

Center and attach the open eye hooks on the top edge of the bin backs. Attach 10" chains with ⅜" screws to the underside of the top, 8" from the front edge and 8" from the sides. Place the bins in the cabinet, with spacers between and on both sides. For smoother movement, sand the notches, if necessary.

APPLY FINISHING TOUCHES. Fill in all voids and countersunk screw holes with wood putty. Finish-sand the cabinet and bins with fine-grit sandpaper. For a finish, choose an enamel with a medium gloss or eggshell finish to make cleaning easy. When the finish is dry, install a metal bin pull on the front of each bin.

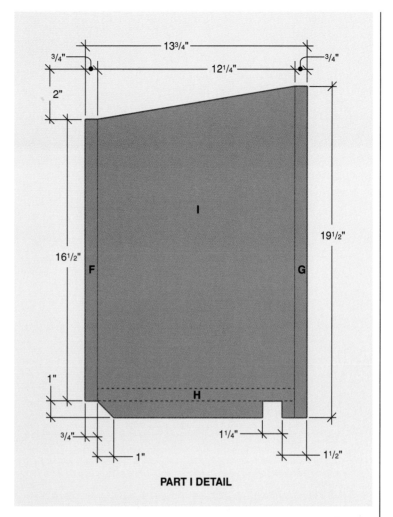

PART I DETAIL

TIP

Ensure a smooth finish by working in a well-ventilated, dust-free area. Airborne dust can ruin a painted finish. Avoid painting a project in an area where woodworking tools have recently operated, and wipe off all sanded surfaces to completely remove dust.

Stepstool

*Make every step a step in the right direction
with our oak stepstool.*

CONSTRUCTION MATERIALS

Quantity	Lumber
1	1 × 10" × 3' oak
1	¾" × 2 × 4' oak plywood

The next time you need to retrieve an out-of-reach item in your kitchen, don't stand on a dining-room chair meant for sitting. Instead, make use of our handy stepstool—it's wide, stable, and reinforced with stretchers underneath each step. The stepstool is just the right height for dusting hard-to-reach areas, like valances and windowtops, and for reaching what you need from that topmost shelf. You'll find the stepstool is also a great place for small children to sit safely out of your way and still feel part of the kitchen "action." The steps are cut from solid oak to guarantee a flat, stable surface. We cut shallow arcs into the bottom of each side panel to create four "feet," and repeated the curves on the front stretchers. A roundover router bit softens the front edges of each step and makes this stool not only handy, but safe as well.

OVERALL SIZE:
14¾" HIGH
16¼" DEEP
17" WIDE

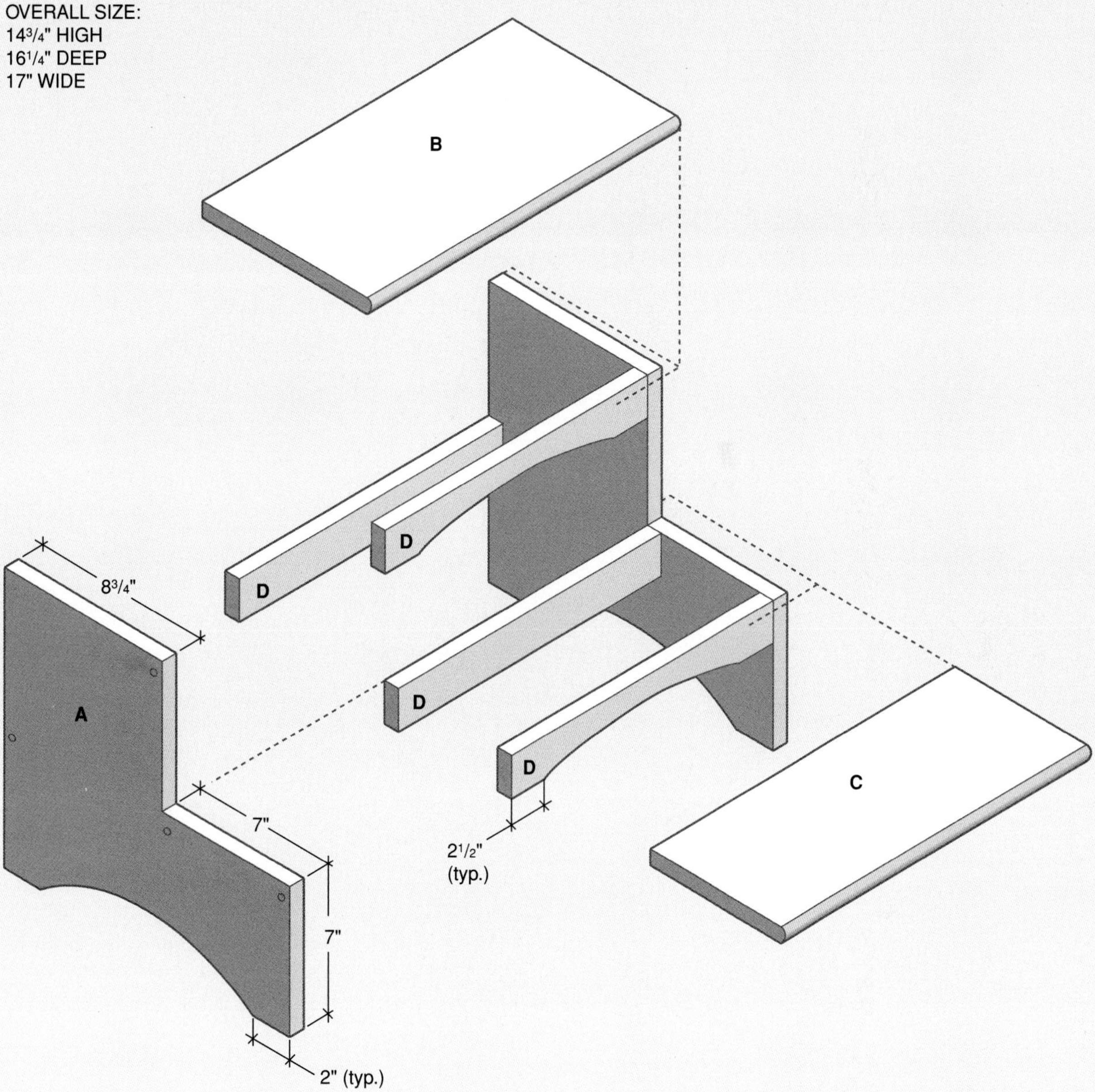

B
D
D
8¾"
A
D
D
7"
7"
2½"
(typ.)
C
2" (typ.)

Cutting List

Key	Part	Dimension	Pcs.	Material
A	Side	¾ × 15¾ × 14"	2	Plywood
B	Top step	¾ × 9¼ × 17"	1	Oak
C	Bottom step	¾ × 7½ × 17"	1	Oak
D	Stretcher	¾ × 2 × 14"	4	Plywood

Materials: Wood glue, wood screws (#8 × 1⅝"), ⅜"-dia. oak wood plugs, oak-veneer edge tape (5'), finishing materials.

Note: Measurements reflect the actual thickness of dimensional lumber.

A

B

A makeshift bar compass achieves smooth, uniform arcs on the front stretchers.

Shorten the compass to draw the arcs on each side piece.

Directions: Stepstool

CUT THE SIDES AND STRETCH-
ERS. Start by cutting the side
pieces (A) and stretchers (D)
to size from oak plywood.
Use a jig saw to cut a 7 × 7"
notch out of one corner on
each side piece, and sand the
cut smooth.

Make the arcs. To achieve
the arched cutouts on the side
pieces and exposed stretchers,
wide-radius arcs are drawn
on each piece with a makeshift
bar compass made from a
pencil, a brad and a thin strip
of wood.

Clamp a stretcher and a
¾"-thick piece of scrap wood at
least 2 ft. long to your worksurface. Draw a centerline across
the width of the stretcher, and
extend the line down the scrap.
Make reference marks 2½" from
each end along the bottom

edge of the stretcher to indicate the ends of the arc. Next,
cut a narrow strip of wood 21½"
long for the arm of the bar
compass. Drill a small hole ½"
in from both ends, one for the
pencil tip, one for the brad.
With the pencil on one of the
reference marks, nail the brad
to the centerline. Then draw
arcs on two of the stretchers
(photo A).

To make the 11¾" arc on the
side pieces, the same process is
employed, but with a shorter
compass. Cut the compass to
10½", and drill a new pencil
hole ½" from the end. Clamp
the side pieces to your worksurface and make reference marks
2" from each corner on the bottom edge of the sides. Position
the compass as done for the
stretchers, nail in place, and
draw arcs on each side piece
(photo B).

Cut all arcs with a jig saw.
Clamp the stretchers together
and gang-sand the cuts smooth
with a drum sander attached
to your drill **(photo C).** Do
the same for the arcs on the
side pieces.

Cut iron-on veneer tape to
length, and apply it to the exposed front and back edges of
the side pieces with an iron
(photo D). To ensure a strong
adhesive bond, press a clean
block of scrap wood against
the strip to flatten the tape
as you go. Let the tape cool,
and trim the edges with a
utility knife.

ASSEMBLE THE FRAME. The
stretchers connect the side
pieces and provide support for
the steps. Position the arched
stretchers between the side
pieces so the edges and corners are flush (see *Diagram*),
and drill counterbored pilot

Clamp the stretchers together and sand the arcs smooth, using a drum sander attached to a drill.

Apply veneer tape to the front and back edges of the side pieces to give them a solid wood appearance.

holes. Attach the side pieces to the stretchers with glue and screws. The two stretchers without arcs are placed at the same height as the lower stretcher. Drill counterbored pilot holes for the remaining stretchers, and attach with wood glue and screws.

CUT AND ATTACH THE STEPS. Cut the top step (B) and bottom step (C) to length from 1 × 10 oak. Rip the bottom step to width. Clamp each step to your worksurface, and round the front edges with a router and a ⅜" roundover bit. Sand the edges smooth.

Position the top step on the assembly so the rear edges are flush and the front overhangs the stretcher by ½". Center the top step from side to side, and drill counterbored pilot holes to connect the step to the side pieces and the

arched stretcher. Apply glue, and drive screws through the holes. Repeat this process for the bottom step.

APPLY FINISHING TOUCHES. Fill all counterbored holes with glued oak plugs, then finish-sand the project. We used two stains for a two-tone look, applying a light cherry stain for the steps and a dark mahogany stain for the side pieces and stretchers. When staining, mask off the edges of the steps where they contact the side pieces and stretchers **(photo E).** If you wish, you can stencil a decorative design on the sides of the stool. Complete the finish with several coats of water-based polyurethane.

Use masking tape to mask off borders where different stains meet.

Cookbook/Recipe Holder

*Keep Grandma's recipe cards and your own cookbooks
together in one handy place.*

CONSTRUCTION MATERIALS

Quantity	Lumber
1	½" × 2 × 4' Baltic birch plywood
1	¼" × 1 × 1' Masonite®

Since kitchens are generally meant for cooking rather than reading, they often lack adequate bookshelf space. But every amateur chef who spends time in a kitchen sooner or later consults a cookbook or two. Our Cookbook/Recipe Holder creates a convenient information center with a small footprint that fits most kitchen countertops. It's designed to keep your favorite cookbooks within easy reach,

but safely out of the way when you really get cookin'. Scalloped details give the project a country flavor. The curved side panels give you easy access but ensure that even oversized cookbooks won't tip. A protective drawer with double pulls shelters your family recipes from messy spattering food. The divided 11½"-wide drawer is the perfect size for holding and organizing hundreds of recipe index cards.

OVERALL SIZE:
17" HIGH
10" DEEP
13" WIDE

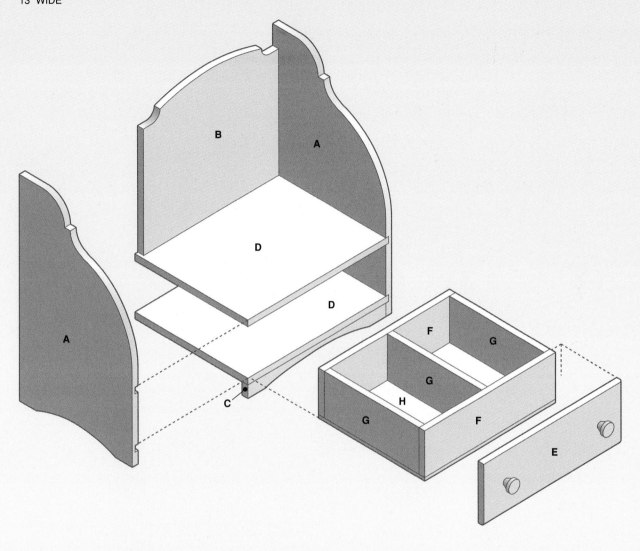

Cutting List

Key	Part	Dimension	Pcs.	Material
A	Side	½ × 10 × 17"	2	Plywood
B	Back	½ × 11 × 12"	1	Plywood
C	Apron	½ × 1 × 12"	1	Plywood
D	Shelf	½ × 10 × 12½ "	2	Plywood

Cutting List

Key	Part	Dimension	Pcs.	Material
E	Drawer front	½ × 4⅝ × 12½"	1	Plywood
F	Drawer end	½ × 3½ × 11¾"	2	Plywood
G	Drawer side	½ × 3½ × 8½ "	3	Plywood
H	Drawer bottom	¼ × 9½ × 11¾"	1	Masonite

Materials: Wood glue, brads (¾", 1"), drawer pulls (2), adhesive rubber feet (4), finishing materials.

Note: Measurements reflect the actual thickness of dimensional lumber.

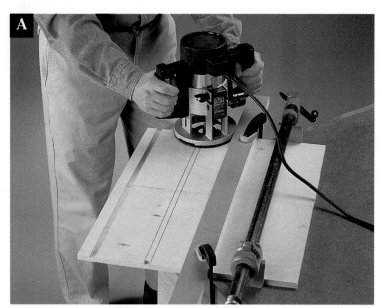

A

Clamp a straightedge to the panel to ensure straight router cuts.

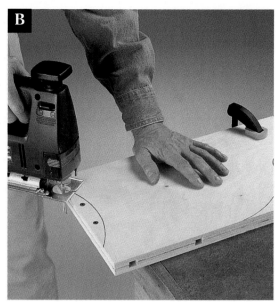

B

Temporarily screw the sides together to gang-cut the scallops.

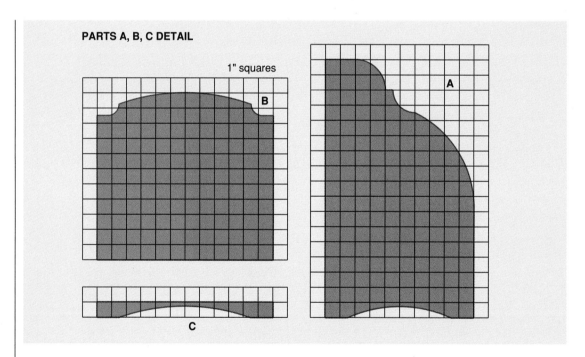

PARTS A, B, C DETAIL

1" squares

B

A

C

Directions: Cookbook/Recipe Holder

MAKE THE SIDES. ½" dadoes cut into the sides hold the shelves in place. To ensure uniformity, both side panels are cut from a single piece of wood after the dadoes are cut. Cut a 20⅛ × 17" piece of plywood. Along the short edges, measure and mark 1", 1½", 5⅜" and 5⅞" up from a long edge. Connect these marks using a straightedge to show the dado paths. Clamp the marked board onto your worksurface and clamp a straightedge or wood scrap as a cutting guide onto the board. Cut the dadoes with a router using a ½" straight bit set to ¼" depth **(photo A).** Next, carefully cut the dadoed board in half creating two identical sides (A). Trace the cutout pattern (see *Diagram*) onto the outside face of one side. Stack the sides together, dadoes facing in, and screw the pieces together through the scrap areas. Clamp the sides to your worksurface and cut out the pattern with a jig saw **(photo B).** Sand the edges smooth.

ASSEMBLE THE PIECES. The shelves house the recipe

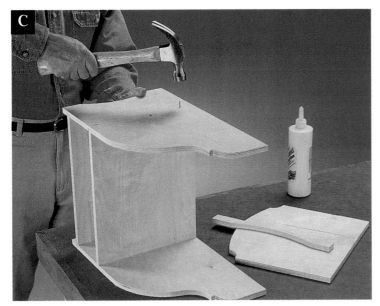

Test-fit the shelves in the dadoes, then attach with glue and brads.

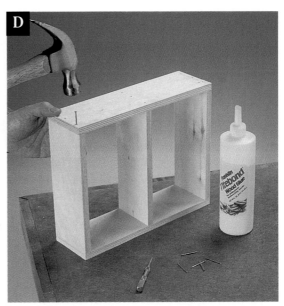

Attach the sides to the drawer ends with glue and brads.

drawer and provide additional top storage space. Cut the back (B), apron (C) and shelves (D) to size. Trace the patterns onto the apron and back (see *Diagram*) and cut with a jig saw. Sand all pieces smooth. Slide the shelves into the dadoes to test-fit and to ensure that the assembly is square. Attach the shelves to the sides with glue and 1" brads **(photo C).** Recess all nail heads with a nail set. Fit the apron, curved side down, between the sides and below the bottom shelf so the corners are flush. Fasten the apron to the sides with glue and brads. Attach the back with glue and brads so the back face is flush with the side edges.

MAKE THE DRAWER. A recipe drawer fits snugly between the shelves. Cut the drawer front (E), drawer ends (F), drawer sides (G) and drawer bottom (H) to size. Sand smooth any rough edges. Place two drawer sides between the drawer ends so the corners are flush. Center the middle drawer side be-

tween the drawer ends to create two compartments (see *Diagram*). Check for squareness. Attach the ends to the sides with glue and 1" brads **(photo D).**

Attach the drawer bottom with glue and brads. Round the outside edges of the drawer front with a belt sander. On the inside of the drawer front, mark reference lines ⅜" from the bottom and sides, and ½" from the top. Position the drawer assembly within these lines, and attach with glue **(photo E).** Clamp the front to the assembly, and secure with ¾" brads driven from inside the assembly.

APPLY FINISHING TOUCHES. Fill all nail heads and any exposed edge grain of the plywood with putty. Finish-sand the entire project, and apply a light enamel paint. Attach screw-on drawer pulls to the drawer front. Place rubber feet on the bottom of the cookbook/recipe holder.

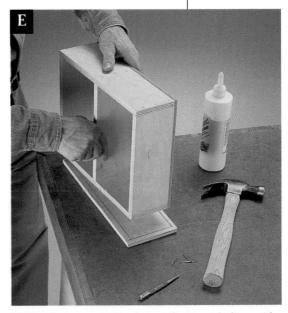

Fit the drawer over the drawer front, and align with the reference lines before attaching.

Cookbook Easel

*The acrylic shield on this easel protects your cookbooks
and lets you concentrate on the cooking.*

CONSTRUCTION MATERIALS

Quantity	Lumber
1	¾" × 2 × 2' basswood handi-panel
1	¼" × 1 × 2' acrylic

Cookbooks are hard to read when covered with flour, batter or tomato sauce. And they tend to take up precious counterspace when open. Our cookbook easel has a removable acrylic shield to protect your favorite cookbooks from messy spatters. The slanted vertical design keeps cookbooks conveniently open and upright, so you can quickly refer to cooking instructions at a glance. The adjustable shield easily accommodates everything from hefty cooking encyclopedias to smaller church cookbooks. Rounded corners add a pleasant touch and soften the overall appearance. To keep the easel from sliding around on the countertop, we added self-adhesive rubber feet to the bottom. With such an efficient design, you could easily make a second easel to protect your Portable Workshop books from shop or garage dust!

OVERALL SIZE:
11½" HIGH
21" WIDE
5½" LONG

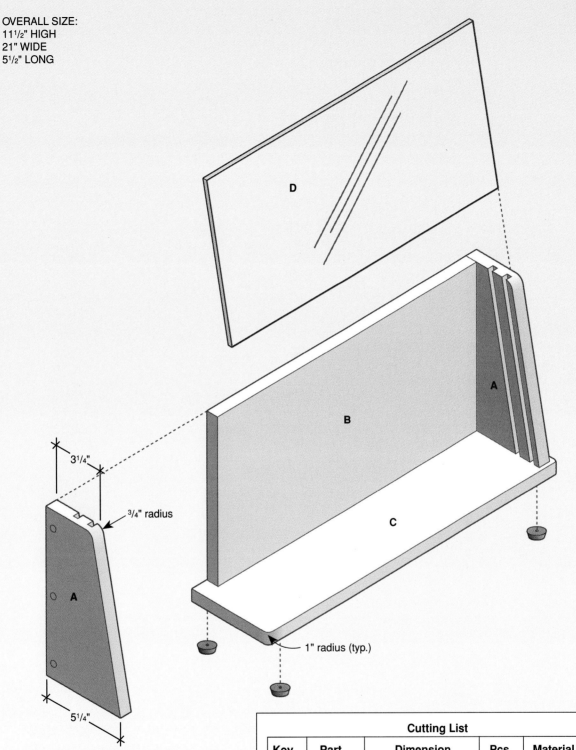

3¼"

¾" radius

A

5¼"

D

B

A

C

1" radius (typ.)

Cutting List				
Key	**Part**	**Dimension**	**Pcs.**	**Material**
A	Side	¾ × 5¼ × 10¼"	2	Basswood
B	Back	¾ × 18¾ × 10¼"	1	Basswood
C	Base	¾ × 5½ × 21"	1	Basswood
D	Shield	¼ × 19¼ × 10¼"	1	Acrylic

Materials: Wood glue, wood screws (#6 × 1½"), self-adhesive rubber feet (4), ⅜"-dia. birch plugs, finishing materials.

Note: Measurements reflect the actual thickness of dimensional lumber.

To make the jig, trace an outline of a side on a piece of plywood and cut with a jig saw.

Draw lines to mark the placement and width of the dadoes.

Directions: Cookbook Easel

MAKE THE SIDES. Cut the sides (A) from ¾" basswood, using a circular saw. The front edge is angled so the side is 5¼" wide at the bottom and 3¼" wide at the top. Sand the cuts smooth with medium-grit sandpaper.

MAKE A JIG FOR ACCURATE DADOES. To make routing the dadoes easier, use a plywood jig to keep the small sides stationary. Place a side on the center of a piece of ¾" scrap plywood and trace its outline. Drill an access hole in the plywood and use a jig saw to make the cut **(photo A).**

CUT THE DADOES. On the inside face of each side, draw parallel lines ⅝", ⅞", 1¾" and 2" from the angled edge

Using a shooting board as a guide, begin and end the dadoes in the plywood jig to avoid any tearouts.

(photo B). These lines mark the location and width of the two dadoes. Next, position the first side in the plywood jig. Align a shooting board on the

plywood so the edge of the shooting board aligns with the marked lines on the side, and temporarily screw in place. Cut the dadoes using a ¼" bit set ⅝"

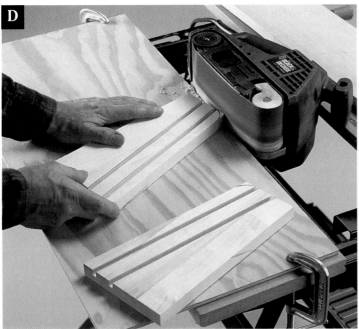

Round the edges on the ends and base with a belt sander.

Find the center of the assembly and mark on the base and back to properly place the screw holes.

deep (to allow for a ⅜"-deep dado and the ¼" shooting board). Begin the router cut in the plywood, proceeding smoothly across the side piece and continuing into the plywood **(photo C).** Reposition the shooting board, and cut the second dado. To make matching cuts in the other side, you must turn the jig over before repeating the above process.

ROUND THE CORNERS. Cut the back (B) and base (C) to size, and sand smooth. Using a compass, draw ¾"-rad. roundovers on the top front corners of the sides and 1"-rad. roundovers on the two front corners of the base. Clamp a belt sander to your worksurface at a 90° angle and round the corners on each part **(photo D).**

ASSEMBLE THE EASEL. All screw holes are counterbored for a finished appearance. To provide stability, the base is slightly larger than the side and back assembly.

Position the back between the sides so the edges are flush, and drill three counterbored pilot holes evenly spaced in the sides. Apply glue to the edges and drive 1½" wood screws through pilot holes into the back. Mark centerpoints on the base and back to help you align the parts correctly **(photo E).** Drill pilot holes in the base and counterbore from the underside. Position the base and back so the centerpoints are aligned and join the base to the assembly with glue and wood screws. (Make sure the screws don't interfere with the dadoes.) Cut the acrylic shield (D) to size with a circular saw, sand the short edges, and insert.

APPLY FINISHING TOUCHES. With a wood mallet, pound glued ⅜" birch plugs into the counterbored holes **(photo F).** Sand the plugs flush with a power sander, and finish-sand the easel. Apply the finish of your choice. (We chose a light

Use a wood mallet to drive in glued ⅜" birch plugs without damaging the surface of the wood.

cherry stain.) Complete the finish with a water-based polyurethane, and attach self-adhesive feet to the base.

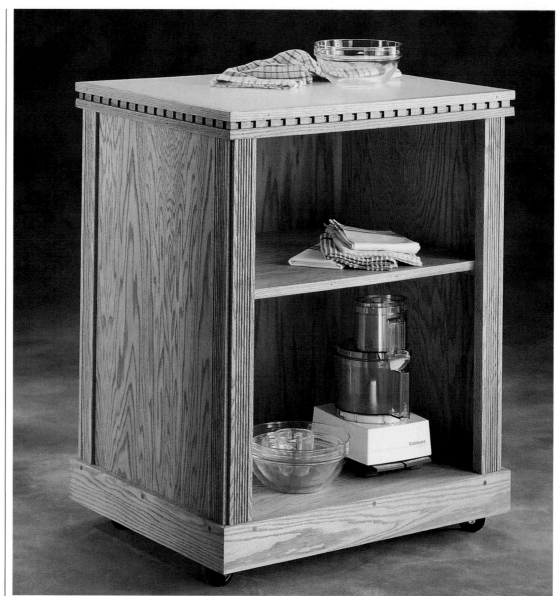

Utility Cart

Form and function combine in this richly detailed rolling cart.

CONSTRUCTION MATERIALS

Quantity	Lumber
2	1 × 2" × 6' oak
2	1 × 4" × 6' oak
1	2 × 4" × 4' pine
1	1 × 4" × 6' pine
1	¾" × 4 × 8' oak plywood
2	⅜ × ⅝" × 6' dentil molding
4	¾ × ¾" × 6' stop molding
8	⅜ × 2¼" × 3' beaded casing
4	¾" × 2 × 3' melamine-coated particleboard

You'll appreciate the extra space, and your guests will admire the classic style of this movable cabinet. The cart features decorative dentil molding around a scratch-resistant 22 × 28½" countertop that provides additional work-surface space for preparing special dishes. Two storage or display areas, framed by banded corner moldings, can hold food, beverages, dinnerware and appliances. Underneath, the cart has casters so it easily rolls across floors to the preparing or serving area. Time and again, you'll find this versatile cart a great help in the kitchen, dining room or other entertainment areas of your home.

OVERALL SIZE:
36" HIGH
30" WIDE
24" DEEP

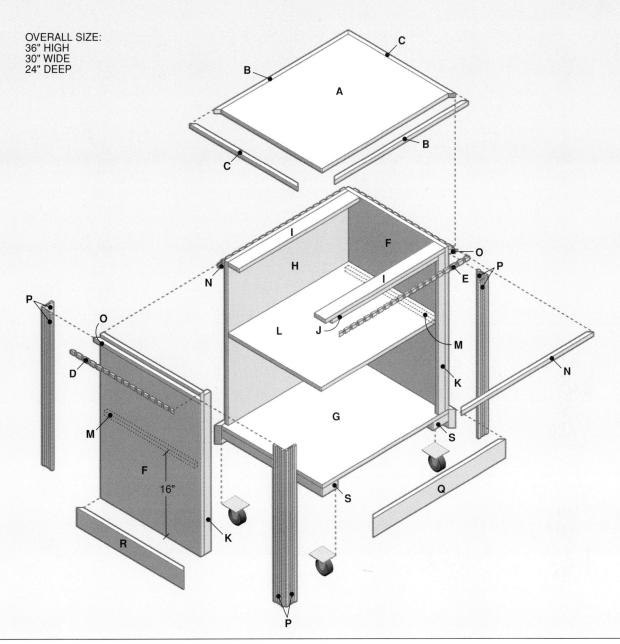

Key	Part	Dimension	Pcs.	Material	Key	Part	Dimension	Pcs.	Material
A	Top	¾ × 22½ × 28½"	1	Particleboard	**K**	Post	¾ × 1½ × 30⅛"	2	Oak
B	Long upper trim	¾ × ¾ × 30"	2	Stop mld.	**L**	Shelf	¾ × 20¾ × 27"	1	Plywood
C	Short upper trim	¾ × ¾ × 24"	2	Stop mld.	**M**	Cleat	¾ × ¾ × 20¼ "	2	Stop mld.
D	Short dentil	⅜ × ⅝ × 23¼"	2	Dentil mld.	**N**	Long lower trim	¾ × ¾ × 30"	2	Stop mld.
E	Long dentil	⅜ × ⅝ × 29¼"	2	Dentil mld.	**O**	Short lower trim	¾ × ¾ × 24"	2	Stop mld.
F	Side panel	¾ × 22½ × 30⅛"	2	Plywood	**P**	Corner trim	⅜ × 2¼ × 29½"	8	Bead. csg.
G	Bottom	¾ × 22½ × 28½"	1	Plywood	**Q**	Long base	¾ × 3½ × 30"	2	Oak
H	Back	¾ × 27 × 30⅞"	1	Plywood	**R**	Short base	¾ × 3½ × 24"	2	Oak
I	Stretcher	¾ × 3½ × 27"	2	Pine	**S**	Caster mount	1½ × 3½ × 22½"	2	Pine
J	Brace	¾ × 1½ × 24"	1	Oak					

Materials: Wood glue, #6 wood screws (1¼", 1⅝", 2"), 4d finish nails, 16-ga. brads, shelf nosing or oak veneer edge tape (30"), 2" casters (4), finishing materials.

Note: Measurements reflect the actual thickness of dimensional lumber.

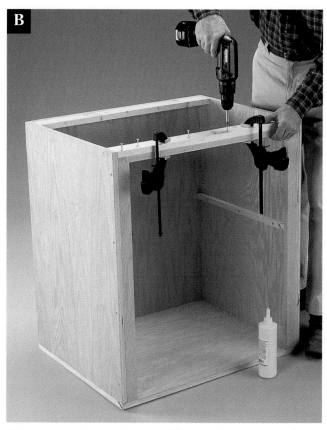

Use a ¾" piece of scrap wood as a spacer to ensure that the cleats are inset ¾" from the edges of the side panels.

Drive screws through the top of the stretcher to secure the oak brace.

Directions: Utility Cart

PREPARE THE SIDES AND BOTTOM. Pilot holes are predrilled into the side panels to make attaching the back and posts easier, and cleats are attached to support the shelf. Start by cutting the side panels (F), bottom (G), back (H) and cleats (M) to size, and sand smooth. Drill four evenly spaced countersunk pilot holes along the long edges of each side panel, ⅜" in from each edge. (Draw a light reference line to help you align the pilot holes.) Flip each side over and, on the inside face, place the cleat so the bottom edge is 16" from the bottom of the side panel. Drill pilot holes and attach the cleat using glue and 1¼" screws. Make sure the ends of the cleats are inset ¾" from the edges of the side panel **(photo A).** Drill countersunk pilot holes along the side and back edges of the bottom as well, but leave the front edge intact.

ASSEMBLE THE CART. Position the back between the side panels, and attach with glue and 1⅝" screws driven through the pilot holes into the back. Attach the bottom panel with glue and screws. Next, cut the stretchers (I), brace (J), posts (K) and shelf (L) to size. Place the stretchers across the top of the cart so the tops are flush at the corners, and attach with glue and 1⅝" screws. Drive screws through the back into the rear stretcher as well. Set the posts in place, faces flush against the side edges, and at-tach with glue and screws driven through the pilot holes in the sides. Apply glue to the brace, and clamp it to the front stretcher. Drive 1¼" screws through the stretcher into the brace **(photo B).** Clamp the shelf vertically to your worksurface. Cut a strip of shelf nosing to match the length of the front edge, apply glue and attach to the shelf. Use wire brads to se-cure the nosing in place **(photo C).** Apply glue to the tops of the cleats, and set the shelf into position inside the cart. Drill pilot holes and nail 4d finish nails through the shelf into the cleats.

ATTACH THE UPPER MOLDING. A series of moldings are fas-tened to the top of the cart, pro-viding a finished look. A miter box and backsaw (or a power

Use glue and brads to attach the shelf nosing in place.

Secure the molding in place with 1" finish nails.

miter box) are useful tools for making the 45° cuts. If you do not have access to a miter box, carefully make the cuts with a jig saw or coping saw. Cut the short dentils (D), long dentils (E), long lower trim pieces (N) and short lower trim pieces (O) to length. Make 45° cuts in the ends of each piece of molding, always angling the cuts inward. When cutting the miters for the dentil molding, make sure to cut through the blocks, or "teeth" of each molding piece so the repeat pattern will match at the corners. Due to variations in dentil molding, you may want to buy extra molding so your pieces align properly. When you've cut the molding, fit the dentil pieces, with the gap edge up, flush to the top edge of the cart. Drill pi-

lot holes for 16-ga. brads, then attach the molding with glue and brads **(photo D).** Attach the lower trim pieces below the dentil molding with brads, and recess all nail heads with a nail set **(photo E).**

ATTACH THE BASE MOLDING. Cut the corner trim (P), long bases (Q), short bases (R) and caster mounts (S) to size. Lay the cart on its back and attach the caster mounts to the bottom of the cart, flush with the bottom edges, using glue and 2" screws. Miter-cut the base pieces, and drill counterbored

pilot holes through the upper part of each base piece. Attach the base pieces with glue and 1¼" screws, making sure the tops of the base pieces are flush with the top edge of the bottom. Apply glue to a corner trim piece and clamp in place over a post so the edges are flush **(photo F).** Drill pilot holes, and secure with finish nails. When the glue is dry, complete the corner by attaching another trim piece with glue and finish nails. The edge of the trim pieces should just touch, but should not overlap. Do this

OPTION

Instead of fastening shelf nosing to the shelf edge, an option is to apply iron-on oak veneer edge tape. Cut the tape to length, and use a household iron to activate the adhesive. When cool, trim away excess tape with a sharp utility knife.

for all four corners, and recess all nail heads with a nail set.

MAKE THE TOP. Mark the dimensions for the top (A) on a piece of melamine-coated particleboard. Apply masking tape over the cut lines, and score them using a straightedge and utility knife **(photo G).** To minimize chip-out when making the cut, use a new or very sharp blade on your circular saw. Cut the top to size, and remove the masking tape. Cut the long upper trim pieces (B) and short upper trim pieces (C) to length, mitering the ends at 45°. Drill pilot holes, and attach the trim pieces with glue and finish nails. Align and center the top over the utility cart, and attach the top with glue and 1¼" screws driven up through the stretchers and into the underside of the top **(photo H).**

APPLY FINISHING TOUCHES. Lay the utility cart on its back, and install the casters. Apply wood putty to all recessed nail heads, and fill the counterbores on the base trim with glued wood plugs. Sand the cabinet smooth, and finish with a stain or sealer of your choice. We used a rustic oak stain to enhance the natural wood appeal.

Attach lower trim underneath the dentil molding, and recess nail heads with a nail set.

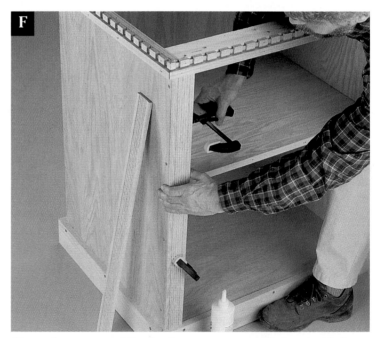

Clamp the corner molding in place to ensure a tight bond with the posts.

G

Score the cut lines on the melamine with a utility knife to make sawing easier.

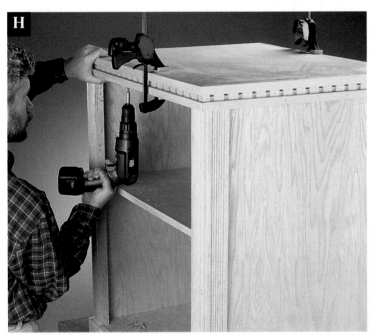

H

Apply glue and clamp the top in place, and secure with screws driven through the brace and stretchers.

TIP

The size of the teeth in dentil molding can vary, as can the gaps between teeth. You might want to purchase extra molding so you can adjust when cutting to get the corners to come out properly.

Cooling Rack

This solid oak cooling rack doubles as a handsome serving tray.

You and your guests will appreciate how well this cooling rack performs. The easy-to-make sculpted openings on the bottom edges of the ends create convenient handholds so you can safely carry fresh-baked foods straight from the oven to the dining table. The rack features efficient ⅜"-dia. oak dowels that allow cooling air to circulate around hot pies, cakes and other baked goods. This versatile 13 × 22" rack is large enough to cool 15 to 20 cookies or two full-size loaves of bread. Yet, the low-profile design lets you easily store or display it on a pantry shelf.

CONSTRUCTION MATERIALS

Quantity	Lumber
1	1 × 3" × 3' oak
1	½ × 2" × 4' oak
13	⅜"-dia. × 24" oak dowels

OVERALL SIZE:
2¹/₂" HIGH
13" WIDE
22" LONG

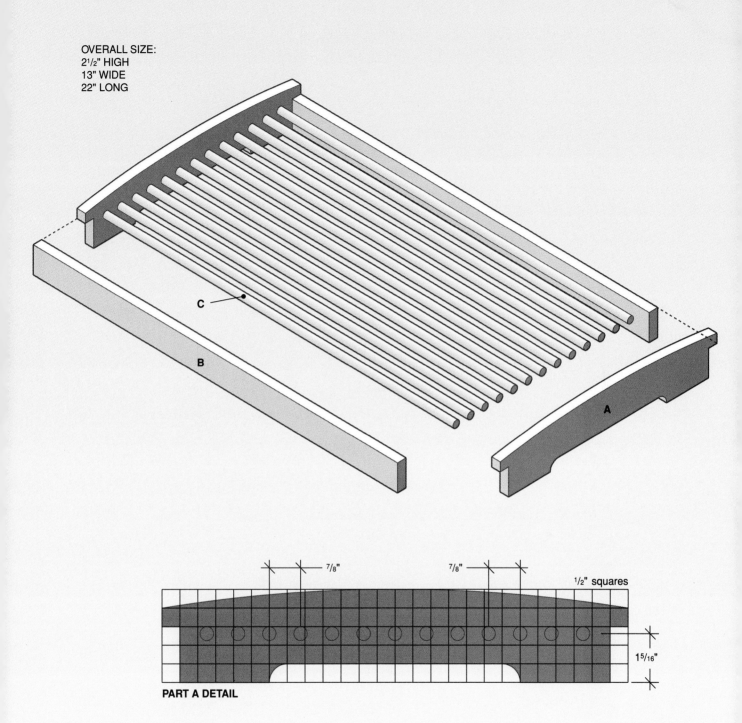

7/8"   7/8"   ¹/₂" squares

1⁵/₁₆"

PART A DETAIL

Cutting List

Key	Part	Dimension	Pcs.	Material
A	End	¾ × 2½ × 13"	2	Oak
B	Side	½ × 1½ × 22"	2	Oak
C	Dowel	⅜ × 21¼"	13	Oak

Materials: Waterproof wood glue, 4d finish nails, finishing materials.

Note: Measurements reflect the actual thickness of dimensional lumber.

Mark the position of the dowel holes and use a drill guide set to ⅜" to drill holes of uniform depth.

Clamp the two ends together at their bases and use a 1" spade bit to drill the arches on the cutouts.

Directions:
Cooling Rack

DRILL THE DOWEL HOLES. Cut the end pieces (A) to length. On each end piece, measure 1⁵⁄₁₆" up from the bottom edge and draw a reference line parallel to the bottom edge. Next, measure in 1¼" from one end and make a mark on the reference line. This mark is the centerpoint of the first dowel hole. Measure 12 more centerpoints, ⅞" apart along the line. Drill the ⅜"-deep holes using a ⅜" brad-point bit and a drill guide **(photo A).**

SHAPE THE END PIECES. The top edge of each end piece is rounded for decoration, and the bottom is sculpted to serve as a handhold. Draw a reference line lengthwise across each end piece, ½" up from the bottom edge. Next, clamp the end pieces together so the bottom edges are butted and the ends are flush. Use a 1" spade bit to drill holes at the joint where the end pieces meet, 3½" in from each end **(photo B).** Unclamp the pieces, and cut along the reference line connecting the holes, using your jig saw. Sand the cuts and holes smooth with a drum sander attached to your drill. Mark notches on each end piece, drawing reference lines ½" in from each short edge, and 1½" up from the bottom (see *Diagram*). Temporarily screw the end pieces together through

the notch areas. Measure ½" down from each top corner and make a mark on each end. Clamp a belt sander to your worksurface at 90° and gang-sand the top corners down to the ½" marks on the sides **(photo C).** Cut out the notches with a jig saw, and sand smooth.

CUT AND FIT THE DOWELS. Cut the dowels (C), and sand the ends. Dry-fit the dowels into the dowel holes in both end pieces. Clamp the assembly together with bar clamps and measure diagonally, corner to corner, to check for square. With the assembly clamped in place, cut the sides (B) to length and sand smooth **(photo D).** Position the sides against the ends, and drill pilot

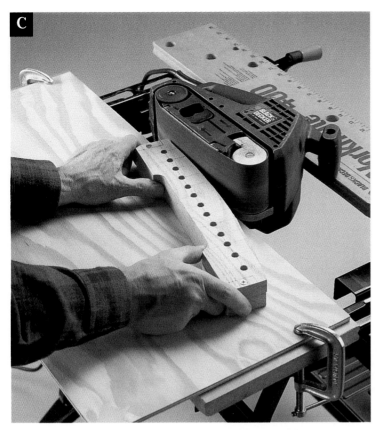

Gang-sand the ends with a belt sander to make matching crowns.

With the assembly still clamped, measure and cut the sides to length.

holes through the sides into the ends. Start 4d finish nails through the pilot holes in each side, and set aside.

ASSEMBLE THE RACK. Once the dowels are fitted, position the sides in the notched areas. Apply waterproof glue to the joints, drive the finish nails into the ends and recess the nails with a nail set.

Apply waterproof glue in each dowel hole, using an artist's brush, and then insert all the dowels into one side **(photo E).** Repeat this process for the other end piece, carefully aligning the dowels. Scrape off excess or visible glue around the dowels, and attach the sides to the ends.

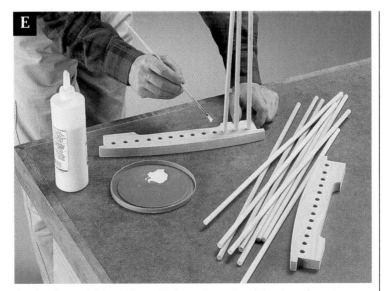

Apply glue quickly and precisely to the ends of the dowels, using an artist's brush.

APPLY FINISHING TOUCHES. Fill the nail holes with putty, and finish-sand the cooling rack with fine-grit sandpaper. If desired, apply a nontoxic finish such as mineral oil.

Paper Towel Holder

*This sturdy dispenser includes a convenient storage shelf
to keep handy items at close reach.*

CONSTRUCTION MATERIALS

Quantity	Lumber
1	¾ × 11 × 48" MDF
1	1"-dia. × 18" oak dowel
1	½"-dia. × 18" oak dowel

*MDF = medium-density fiberboard

Curved ends soften the profile of this paper towel holder and give you better access to the paper towels. The 2½ × 11 × 11½" compartment shelf is great for keeping boxes of foil, plastic wrap, lunch bags and other frequently used dry goods within easy reach. Replacing the paper towel rolls is a simple matter of withdrawing the 1" oak rod.

Though it is ideally suited for kitchen use, you may want to build several of these heavy-duty units to use in your basement, garage and laundry area. With ¾"-thick sides, shelf and a large 11 ×17½" base, it will stand up to years of use, even when mounted in a high-traffic area. And if left unmounted on a countertop or workbench, this paper towel holder is heavy enough to resist sliding and tipping.

OVERALL SIZE:
9³/₄" HIGH
17¹/₂" WIDE
11" DEEP

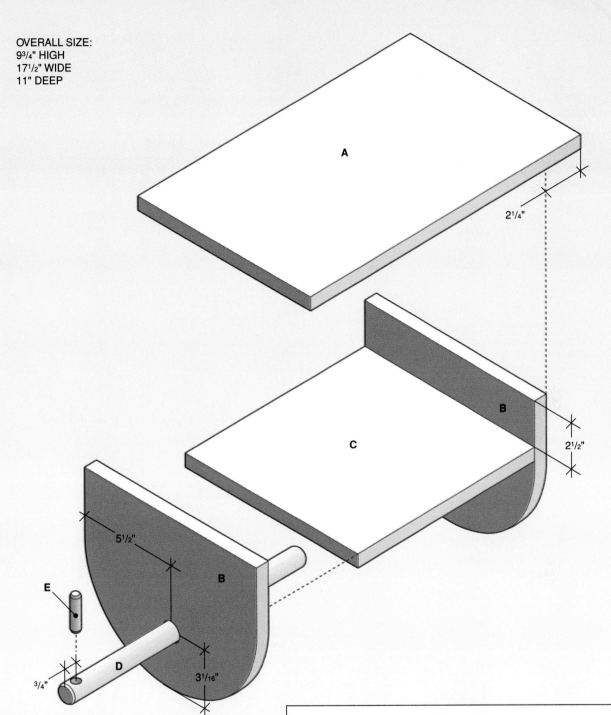

Cutting List				
Key	**Part**	**Dimension**	**Pcs.**	**Material**
A	Top	¾ × 11 × 17½"	1	MDF
B	End	¾ × 11 × 9¼"	2	MDF
C	Shelf	¾ × 11 × 11½"	1	MDF
D	Rod	1"-dia. × 15"	1	Oak dowel
E	Stop dowel	½"-dia. × 2"	1	Oak dowel

Materials: Wood glue, #6 × 1½" screws, 4d finish nails, putty, finishing materials.

Note: Measurements reflect the actual thickness of dimensional lumber.

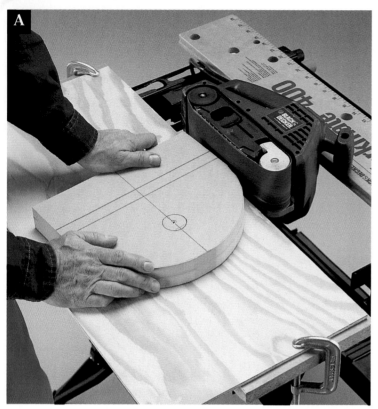

A

B

Temporarily screw the two end pieces together through the center-point of the dowel rod hole, and finish the curves with a belt sander.

Drill through ends into scrap plywood to make clean holes and to protect your worksurface.

Directions:
Paper Towel Holder

MAKE THE ENDS. Begin by cutting the end blanks (B) to size. On each end, mark the shelf location and the center-point for the rod holes and semicircles (see *Diagram*). Use a compass set to a 3¹⁄₁₆" radius to draw the curves.

To ensure that both end pieces are identical, screw them together at the center-point of the rod hole, then cut both ends at the same time with a jig saw. Belt-sand the two ends smooth while they are still secured together **(photo A).** Unscrew the pieces and drill the rod hole through each end, using a 1⅛"-dia. spade bit **(photo B).**

ASSEMBLE THE SHELF AND TOP. Cut the top (A) and shelf (C) to size, and sand smooth. Drill countersunk pilot holes for attaching the top to the ends. (If you will be mounting the holder to a cabinet, also drill countersunk pilot holes through the bottom face of the top piece, in the areas where the top will overhang the end pieces.) Also drill pilot holes through the ends where the shelf will be attached with finish nails. Join the shelf and ends with glue and 4d finish nails. Attach the top with glue and 1½" wood screws.

CUT THE ROD AND DOWEL. To hold the rod firmly in place while drilling the hole for the stop dowel, build a simple V-jig by using your circular saw to cut a V-shaped notch across the middle of an 18"-long piece of 2 × 8. Set your saw blade at a 45° angle to cut the V-notch **(photo C).**

Cut the oak rod (D) and stop dowel (E) to length. Measure and mark a centerpoint ¾" in from one end of the rod. Clamp the rod onto the V-jig and use a portable drill guide to drill the ½" stop dowel hole through the centerpoint **(photo D).**

TIP:

To drill straight holes into dowels and rods, make sure your portable drill guide rests flat on the 2 × 8 sides of the V-jig. To make your V-jig more stable, mount it onto a larger piece of ¾" plywood.

With your saw set to 1½" depth, make two 45° cuts across the middle of an 18" length of 2 × 8 to create a V-jig.

Clamp rod in V-jig and support portable drill guide on the flat sides of the 2 × 8 to create a straight hole.

Clamp your belt sander on its side on your worksurface, then clamp or nail a scrap piece of wood close to the belt, at an angle of about 45°. Apply a strip of tape ⅛" from each end of the dowel, then rest the dowel against the angled guide and *chamfer* (bevel) each end of the dowel by rotating it against the spinning belt **(photo E).** Also chamfer the stop dowel ends in the same fashion, then glue it into the oak rod.

APPLY FINISHING TOUCHES. Recess all nail heads using a nail set, and fill the holes with putty. Sand the entire unit to 150-grit smoothness, and apply the paint of your choice. If you are mounting the holder underneath a cabinet, attach it with screws driven through the pilot holes in the top.

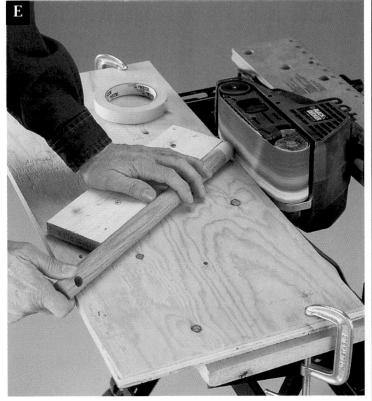

Use a mounted belt sander and an angle guide made from a block of wood screwed to a plywood base to create precise chamfers.

Silverware Caddy

*This decorative display rack brings convenience
to dinnertime chores.*

Silverware caddies used to be common accessories on the prairie years ago, when large family gatherings were regular occurrances. A caddy eliminated lugging handfuls of silverware to and from the table, made setting the table a speedy chore and kept utensils ready at attention for the next meal. Our silverware caddy is crafted from traditional, sturdy oak and features a decorative cloverleaf carrying grip. The rounded handle and divider interlock, creating four sections to keep knives, spoons and dinner and salad forks separate and upright for easy identification. Perfect for displaying your good silver, this is an easy afternoon project that will give long-lasting "service" to any dinner table.

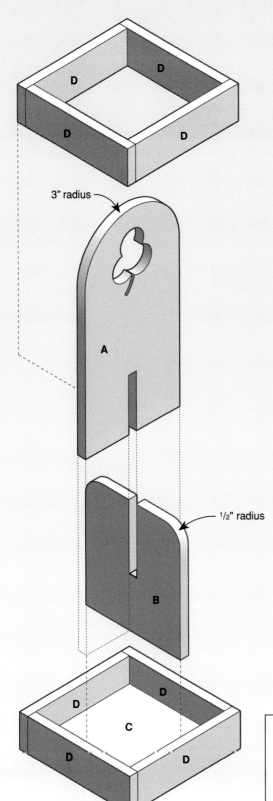

OVERALL SIZE:
12½" HIGH
7" WIDE
7" LONG

3" radius

½" radius

½" squares

PART A DETAIL

Cutting List

Key	Part	Dimension	Pcs.	Material
A	Handle	½ × 6 × 12"	1	Oak
B	Divider	½ × 6 × 6"	1	Oak
C	Base	½ × 6 × 6"	1	Oak
D	Side	½ × 2 × 6½"	8	Oak

Materials: Wood glue, 16-ga. 1" finish nails, finishing materials.

Note: Measurements reflect the actual thickness of dimensional lumber.

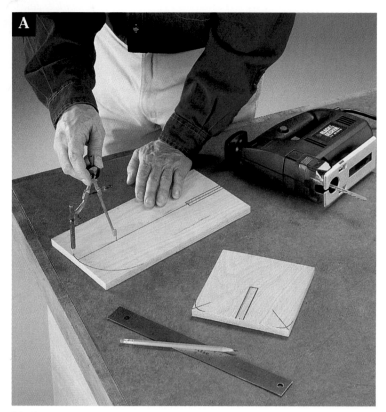

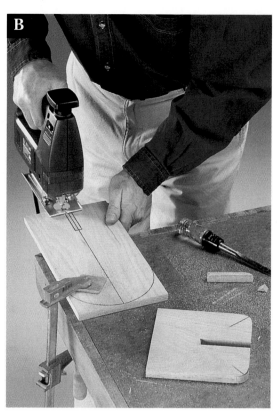

Mark curves and notch locations on reference lines using a compass.

Clamp pieces to your worksurface to ensure steady cuts.

Directions:
Silverware Caddy

MAKE THE HANDLE AND DI-VIDER. Corners on the handle and divider are curved, and the pieces are notched to fit together. Start by cutting the handle (A) and divider (B) to size. Mark a centerline down the length of each piece, and draw a ½ × 3" notch at one end centered along each line. At the other end of the handle, place a compass point on the centerline, 3" from the edge, and draw a 3"-rad. curve. At the notched end of the divider, bi-sect each corner with a 45° line. Place a compass point on the 45° line ¹¹⁄₁₆" from the corner, and draw ½"-rad. curves on each corner **(photo A).** Clamp each piece to your worksur-face, and cut the curves and

notches with a jig saw **(photo B).** Slide the notched ends to-gether to test-fit, and use a chisel to clean out the notches and make adjustments.

CUT THE HANDHOLD. A deco-rative cloverleaf cutout pro-vides a handhold for the silverware caddy. Transfer the clover template (see *Diagram*) to paper, and trace the pattern onto the handle surface, using the centerline for correct align-ment. Cut out each "leaf" of the clover with a 1½"-dia. hole saw **(photo C).** Keep a scrap piece of wood underneath to prevent the hole saw tearing through the other side of the handle. Cut out the clover stem with a

jig saw and chisel. Sand all cuts to remove splinters, and sand the inside of the clover smooth with a 1"-dia. or smaller drum sander attached to your drill **(photo D).**

ASSEMBLE THE BASE AND SIDES. The handle and divider fit together into a base assem-bly. Cut the sides (D) and base (C) to size, and sand smooth. To make the side frames square, each side end should butt against the face of another side (see *Diagram*). Drill pilot holes at the side joints to ease assembly. Glue and nail four sides together with finish nails and repeat to make two square frames. Check for square when

---

TIP

When predrilling and nailing the frames of the silverware caddy, angle, or "toenail" each pair of nails toward the middle to provide a stronger joint.

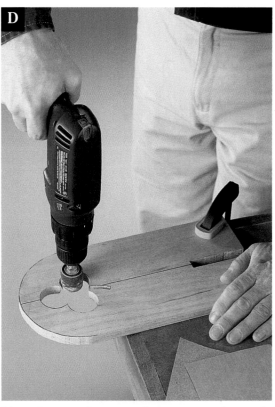

A hole saw cuts quickly and cleanly. Use a backer board underneath to prevent tearouts on the other side of handle.

Use a drum sander, or sandpaper wrapped around a dowel, to smooth the inside of the cutout.

nailing, then recess all nail heads with a nail set. Place the base inside one of the frames, drill pilot holes and attach the base with glue and nails. Set the handle and divider inside to test-fit, then apply glue to the joint. Attach the handle and divider to the base assembly with glue and finish nails. Slide the remaining frame over the handle and divider. Keep a 1¼" gap between frames, and attach the frame to the handle and divider with glue and finish nails **(photo E).**

APPLY FINISHING TOUCHES. Fill all nail holes with wood putty. Sand smooth, and apply the finish of your choice. We used a light cherry stain. If you choose paint, use a nontoxic interior-rated latex enamel.

Maintain a 1¼" gap between frames when assembling.

PROJECT
POWER TOOLS

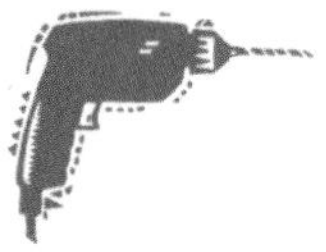

Kitchen Island

Our stand-alone cabinet and countertop island expands the versatility of any kitchen.

Construction Materials

Quantity	Lumber
7	⅝" × 2 × 4' pine panel
4	1 × 2" × 8' pine
1	1 × 4" × 4' pine
1	2 × 8" × 2' pine
4	¾ × ¾" × 8' pine stop molding
1	¾" × 4 × 4' particleboard
1	¼" × 4 × 4' tileboard

This project is a great-looking alternative to more expensive custom cabinetry, and every bit as useful. The kitchen island gives you additional space for preparing food, as well as a convenient spot to enjoy a light snack or a quick meal. The ends, back panels and shelves are constructed from edge-glued ponderosa pine, a convenient building material that provides a distinctively appealing pattern for cabinetry. The front of the island sports a finished face frame and features adjustable shelving for dishes or other cooking utensils. The countertop has an 8" overhang and provides room for two to sit comfortably.

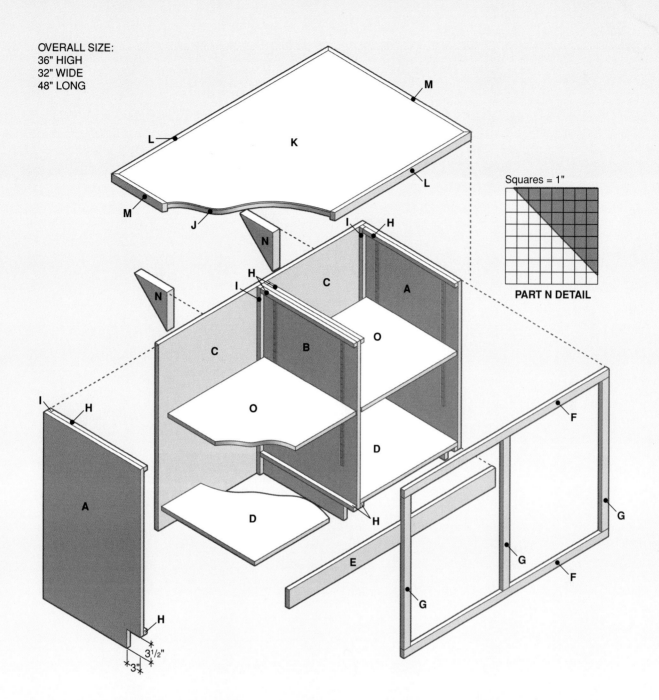

OVERALL SIZE:
36" HIGH
32" WIDE
48" LONG

Squares = 1"

PART N DETAIL

Key	Part	Dimension	Pcs.	Material
A	End	⅝ × 21½ × 35"	2	Pine panel
B	Divider	⅝ × 21½ × 35"	1	Pine panel
C	Back	⅝ × 22⅛ × 35"	2	Pine panel
D	Bottom	⅝ × 21⅛ × 21½"	2	Pine panel
E	Toe board	¾ × 3½ × 44¼"	1	Pine
F	Rail	¾ × 1½ × 44¼"	2	Pine
G	Stile	¾ × 1½ × 28½"	3	Pine
H	Horiz. cleat	¾ × ¾ × 20¾"	8	Molding

Key	Part	Dimension	Pcs.	Material
I	Vert. cleat	¾ × ¾ × 35"	4	Molding
J	Substrate	¾ × 30½ × 46½"	1	Particleboard
K	Top	¼ × 30½ × 46½"	1	Tileboard
L	Long edge	¾ × 1½ × 48"	2	Pine
M	Short edge	¾ × 1½ × 32"	2	Pine
N	Support	1½ × 7¼ × 7¼"	2	Pine
O	Shelf	⅝ × 20½ × 20½"	2	Pine panel

Cutting List

Materials: Wood glue, #6 wood screws (1", 1¼", 1½"), ½" tacks, 4d finish nails, 24" shelf standards (8), shelf standard supports, contact cement, finishing materials.

Cut the toe board notches into the ends and divider using a jig saw.

Gang the cleats together while drilling countersunk pilot holes.

Directions: Kitchen Island

CUT THE ENDS AND DIVIDER. Cut the ends (A) and divider (B) to size from pine panels, using a circular saw. Measure and mark the 3"-wide × 3½"-tall toe board notches on the lower front corners of all three pieces using a combination square (see *Diagram*). This notch and the toe board provide a *kick space*, allowing you to approach a cabinet without stubbing your toes against the bottom. Clamp each piece to your worksurface, and cut out the toe board notches using a jig saw **(photo A).**

PREPARE THE CLEATS. The cleats reinforce the internal joints of the cabinet. Countersunk pilot holes are drilled through each cleat in two directions, and are offset so the screws won't hit one another.

Cut the horizontal cleats (H) and the vertical cleats (I) to length from ¾ × ¾" stop molding. Clamp the vertical cleats together so the ends are flush, and mark four pilot hole locations along the length of each cleat (see *Detail* for pilot hole locations). Place the clamped cleats on a piece of scrap plywood, and drill countersunk pilot holes at each marked location. Remove the clamps and give each cleat a quarter turn. Reclamp the cleats, then mark and drill the second set of offset pilot holes. Repeat the process for the horizontal cleats, drilling three holes through one edge of each cleat and two offset holes through an adjacent edge **(photo B).**

ASSEMBLE THE ENDS AND DIVIDER. Align a vertical cleat along the inside back edge of

PARTS H AND I DETAIL

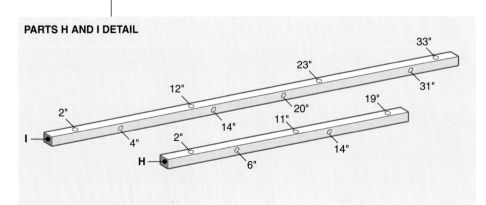

Center a marked template between the cleats to uniformly attach the shelf standards.

Clamp the back to the divider along the centerline, and adjust when attaching to the end.

one of the ends. Align the pilot holes so the back can be attached through the offset holes. Apply glue and fasten the cleat to the end with counter-sunk 1" screws. Attach vertical cleats to the inside face of the other end, and to both back edges of the divider. Attach the horizontal cleats to the ends and divider, using glue and 1" screws.

ATTACH THE SHELF STAN-DARDS. The shelf standards are positioned on the ends and divider with the aid of a simple template. Cut a 15 × 30" template from scrap particleboard or heavy-stock cardboard. Make sure the standards are properly aligned in the same direction so the holes for the supports uniformly line up. Place the template on the lower horizontal cleat, and cen-

ter the template between the vertical cleat and the front edge. Measure 2" up from the bottom edge along each side of the template and make a reference mark. Place a standard against each edge of the template and adjust so the bottom of the standard is on the 2" mark. Nail the standards in place with ½" tacks. Do the same on the other end, and on

both faces of the divider **(photo C).**

ASSEMBLE THE CABINET. Cut the backs (C), bottoms (D) and toe board (E) to size, and sand the edges smooth. Cut ¾ × ¾" notches in the back corners of each bottom to accommodate the vertical cleats.

Stand one end and the divider upright on their front edges. Then position a bottom

---

TIP

The back, end, divider, bottom and shelf pieces used in this project are constructed from ⅝" edge-glued ponderosa pine panels, available at most building centers. This material, available in varying dimensions and thicknesses, is manufactured from small-width pine glued together under pressure. The result is a strong material that is slightly thinner than standard dimensional plywood. It features a distinctive paneled appearance, and since it is made entirely of one type of wood, exposed edges do not require veneer.

Arrange the toe board so the corners and edges are flush, and attach to the divider and ends with glue and 4d finish nails.

Sand the rails after the stiles to avoid cross-sanding marks on the rails.

piece against the lower horizontal cleats. Use bar clamps to hold the assembly in place, and attach the bottom with glue and 1" screws driven through the pilot holes in each cleat. Position the remaining bottom and end in place, and attach the bottom to the cleats.

Attach the back pieces one at a time, using glue and 1" screws driven through the vertical cleats inside the cabinet. Make sure each back piece is aligned with its inside edge flush against a marked reference centerline on the divider. Check frequently for square, and use pipe clamps to hold the pieces in position as you attach them **(photo D).**

Carefully turn the assembly over, and fasten the toe board in place with glue and 4d finish nails.

ASSEMBLE THE FACE FRAME. Cut the rails (F) and stiles (G) to size, and sand them smooth. Position the top rail so the top edges and corners are flush, and attach with glue and finish nails. Attach the stiles so the outside edges are flush with the end faces and centered on the divider. Finally, attach the bottom rail **(photo E).** Reinforce the joints by drilling pilot holes through the rails into the ends of each stile and securing with 4d finish nails. Use an orbital sander to smooth the face frame and the joints between

stiles and rails. By sanding the stiles before the rails, you can avoid cross-sanding marks at the joints **(photo F).**

BUILD THE COUNTERTOP. Cut the substrate (J), top (K), long edges (L) and short edges (M) to size. Make sure the top fits perfectly over the substrate, and trim if necessary. Miter-cut the ends of the long edges and short edges at 45° angles to fit around the countertop.

Apply contact cement to the substrate, and clamp the top in place, using scrap wood under the clamps to distribute pressure and ensure even contact with the cement **(photo G).**

When dry, unclamp and flip the assembly on its top. Arrange

Clamping scrap boards to the tileboard helps distribute pressure and evens contact.

Attach the supports to the back from inside the cabinet using glue and screws.

the long and short edges around the countertop, so the top surface will be flush with the tops of the edge pieces. Glue and clamp the edges in place. Drill pilot holes and drive 4d finish nails through the edges into the substrate.

ATTACH THE COUNTERTOP AND SHELVES. Cut the shelves (O) from pine panels. Cut the supports (N) from 2 × 8 dimensional pine. (A single 7¼ × 7¼" piece cut diagonally will create these supports.) Break the cut corners at the ends of each diagonal, using a jig saw or a sander. This softens the profile of the supports and reduces the chance of snagged clothing under the countertop.

To attach the supports, mark a line on the top edge of the back, 11" in from each end. Position the supports so they are centered on the lines. Then drill pilot holes through the back and attach the supports with glue and 1½" screws driven from the inside of the cabinet **(photo H).**

Center the countertop from side to side on the cabinet with a 1" overhang on the front. Attach with glue and 1¼" screws driven up through the top horizontal cleats. Insert supports into the shelf standards at the desired height, and install the shelves inside the cabinet with the grain running left to right.

APPLY FINISHING TOUCHES. Recess all visible nail heads with a nail set, and fill the holes with putty. Sand all surfaces, outer edges and corners smooth. Finish the kitchen island with a light stain (we used a traditional American pine finish), and apply a nontoxic topcoat.

Trivet

Protect your countertops, tables and furniture during teatime with our Colonial-style trivet.

You'll love this easy-to-construct trivet. Its intricate trim and arched legs make it a popular conversation piece during teatime.

The heavy tile stabilizes the base, making it ideal for keeping teapots off your favorite furniture or serving cart. For this project, we selected a standard Colonial oak trim pattern to make the arched legs and a neutral-color tile for the base, but you can customize this trivet by using any color of tile that matches your tea set or suits your taste. Our basic design features a single 12 × 12" tile cut down to a finished size of 6 × 9". Using one tile is a simple method that doesn't

require grout. But you will find it easy to adapt this design for smaller tiles or mosaic tiles that do require grout: simply match the size of the substrate to the finished dimensions of the tile-and-grout surface (including a grout border between the tiles and the oak frame), and cut the oak molding pieces accordingly. The construction steps remain the same.

CONSTRUCTION MATERIALS

Quantity	Lumber
1	¾" × 2 × 2' MDF
1	⅝ × 2¼" × 4' oak molding
1	¼ × 12 × 12" tile

MDF = medium-density fiberboard

OVERALL SIZE:
2¼" HIGH
7⁵/₁₆" WIDE
10⁵/₁₆" LONG

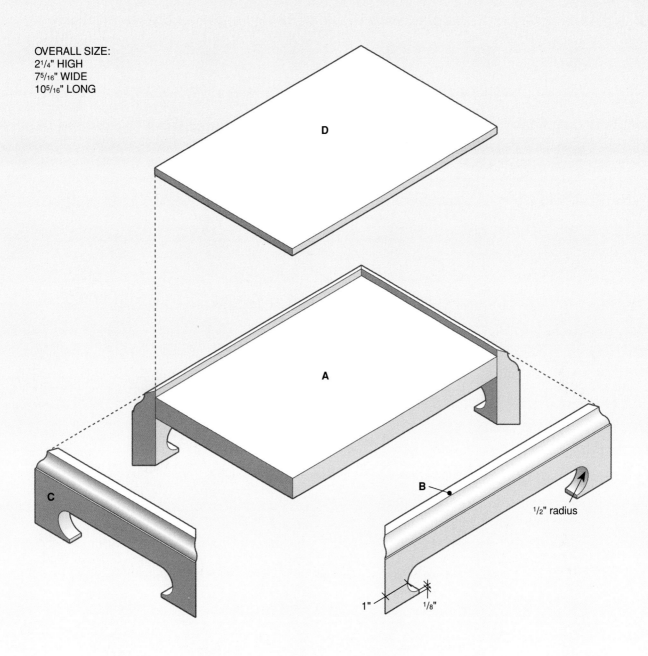

½" radius

1"   ⅛"

Cutting List

Key	Part	Dimension	Pcs.	Material
A	Substrate	¾ × 6 × 9"	1	MDF
B	Side	⅝ × 2¼ × 10⁵/₁₆"	2	Oak molding
C	End	⅝ × 2¼ × 5⁵/₁₆"	2	Oak molding
D	Tile	¼ × 6 × 9"	1	Ceramic tile

Materials: Waterproof wood glue, tile adhesive, 1" brads, finishing materials. (Optional: grout, clear silicone caulk.)

Note: Measurements reflect the actual thickness of dimensional lumber.

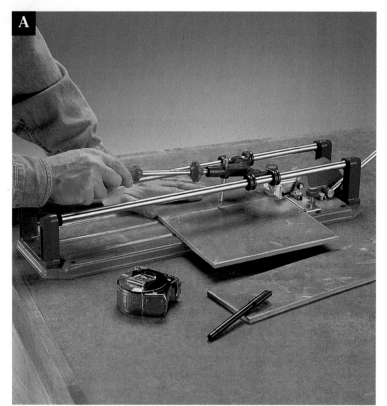

A

B

Use a tile cutter to make fast, clean cuts on ceramic tile.

Test-fit the base molding side and end pieces to the substrate and tile before applying glue.

Directions: Trivet

CUT THE TILE AND SUBSTRATE. We've found a 12 × 12" tile cut to 6 × 9" is a convenient size for a trivet. It is large enough to hold a good-sized teapot, yet small enough to handle easily. Select your tile (D), then mark and cut it to the correct size with a tile cutter **(photo A).** If you don't have a tile cutter, clamp the tile to your worksurface and cut it using a rod saw (similar to a coping saw, but with an abrasive blade designed for cutting tile). Measure and cut the substrate (A) to match the finished tile size.

CUT THE MOLDING. Cut the sides (B) and ends (C) to length from the base molding. Make 45° miter cuts at the ends of each piece.

ATTACH MOLDING TO SUBSTRATE. Place the tile facedown on the worksurface and position the substrate, bottom side up, over the tile. Test-fit each side and end against the substrate. Scribe a line along the edge of the substrate to mark where the substrate joins the molding **(photo B).** Apply waterproof glue to the sides and ends, and attach them to the substrate so the reference marks are aligned. With the tile temporarily in place, fasten a band clamp around the perimeter at the line where substrate edges meet the base molding **(photo C).** After the glue dries, remove the band clamp and the tile. Drill pilot holes through the molding into the substrate. Secure the molding with 1" brads, and recess the nail heads with a nail set.

CREATE THE LEGS. Legs are formed by cutting holes in the molding near each corner joint. Along the bottom edges of each side and end, measure in 1½" inches from each corner and ⅝" up from the bottom edge. This is the centerpoint for each hole. Construct a small support jig/backer board to fit inside the skirt formed by the base molding. For a 6 × 9" tile inset, a 6 × 9" piece of scrap will do. Attach the jig to the bench so it overhangs the edge. Place the trivet on the jig, and drill holes at each centerpoint with a 1" spade bit **(photo D).** Be careful that you drill only through the sides and ends, and not into the substrate. Draw a connecting line between the tops of each set of

Use a band clamp to hold base and ends in contact with the substrate while glue dries.

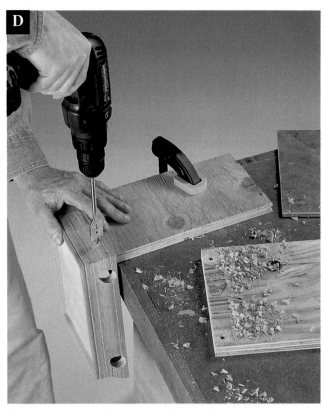

Use scrap plywood to support trivet and prevent tearouts while drilling "leg" holes in the molding.

holes, and cut along this line with your jig saw. Complete each cutout by cutting straight up from the bottom edge into the center of each hole **(photo E).**

SAND AND FINISH. Sand the cutout edges with 150-grit sandpaper, making sure to round the sharp edges on the bottom of the legs. Finish the trivet as desired.

ATTACH THE TILE. Apply an even coat of tile adhesive to the top of the substrate, and set the tile into the base. Depending on the width of the gap between the molding and the tile on the finished piece, you may want to fill it with a clear silicone caulk to prevent moisture or crumbs from collecting. If you selected mosaic tiles for this project, mask the sides of

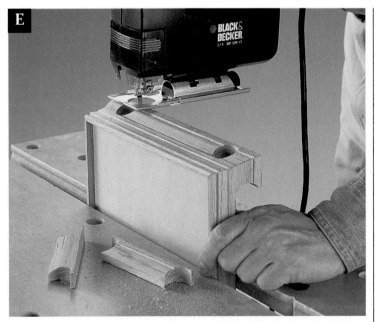

Clamp the trivet to your worksurface, and carefully cut out the legs, using a jig saw.

the base before grouting to protect the molding and apply a silicone grout sealer when fin-

ished to prevent stains from penetrating the grout.

Serving Tray

*Smooth joinery and sturdy construction
make serving food and beverages a snap.*

CONSTRUCTION MATERIALS

Quantity	Lumber
1	½ × 3¾" × 2' oak "hobby wood"
1	½ × 2¾" × 3' oak "hobby wood"
1	¼ × 12" × 2' birch plywood

Our serving tray is just the thing for ferrying food, drinks and dishes from kitchen to patio or dining room with a dash of style. The solid oak and warm birch tones of the tray always highlight whatever you're carrying, whether an outdoor snack of fruit and cheese or an indoor treat of coffee and cookies. The sculpted carrying handles ensure a sure grip while carrying food to your guests. The serving tray is also an introduction to some advanced joinery techniques. Rabbet joints connect the frame to provide a more professional-looking appearance. The bottom panel fits into dadoes cut along the inside of each piece, and stays in place without glue. This is a great project for practicing router skills, or for showing them off if you're an accomplished woodworker.

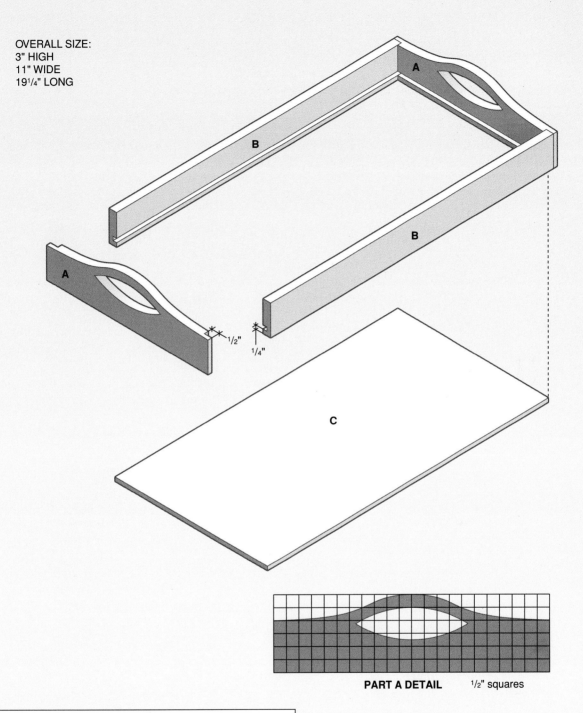

OVERALL SIZE:
3" HIGH
11" WIDE
19¼" LONG

A

B

A

B

½"

¼"

C

PART A DETAIL   ½" squares

Cutting List				
Key	**Part**	**Dimension**	**Pcs.**	**Material**
A	Frame end	½ × 3 × 11"	2	Oak
B	Frame side	½ × 2 × 18¾"	2	Oak
C	Tray bottom	¼ × 10⅜ × 18⅝"	1	Birch

Materials: Wood glue, 4d finish nails, finishing materials.
Optional: ⅜" stop molding (5'), brads (½", ¾").

Note: Measurements reflect the actual thickness of
dimensional lumber.

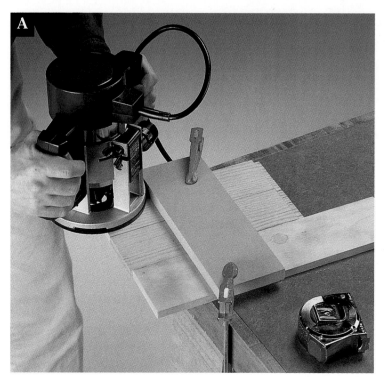

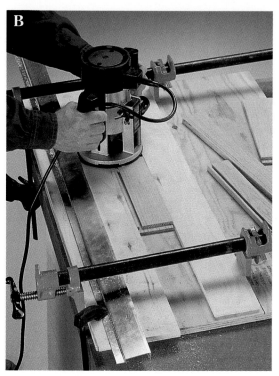

Continue the rabbet cuts into a piece of scrap to avoid tearouts.

Use bar clamps and a straightedge to hold pieces in place and ensure uniform dadoes.

Directions: Serving Tray

MAKE THE RABBETS. The corners of the tray feature ½" rabbet joints for strength and a unified look.

Measure and cut the frame ends (A) to length. Place the frame ends side by side on your worksurface with their ends aligned, and butt them against a scrap piece of ¾"-thick wood placed to the right of them. (Continuing each rabbet cut into the scrap wood helps prevent tearouts.) Place a straight board or straightedge over the frame ends to guide your cut, align the board and clamp in place. Use a ½" straight-cutting router bit set ¼" deep, and rabbet the two frame ends, completing the cut into the scrap board **(photo A).** Cut rabbets on both ends of the tray ends.

MAKE THE DADOES. Dadoes are cut in the frame sides and frame ends to secure the tray bottom in place. A simple jig is used to help make uniform, straight dadoes.

Cut the frame sides (B) to size, and sand smooth. Draw parallel lines ¼" and ½" from the bottom edges of the frame sides and frame ends to mark the dadoes. Create a cutting jig by clamping two pieces of ¾" scrap wood against the long edges of a frame side. Clamp a straightedge over the board to guide the router base while cutting the long dadoes. Make the dadoes in both frame sides with a ¼" straight-cutting router bit set ¼" deep **(photo B).** Adjust the clamps, and dado the frame ends in the same fashion.

OPTION: If you don't want to cut dadoes, you can support the tray bottom with cleats made from ⅜" stop molding. Cut the cleats to fit inside the tray, and attach them flush to the bottom edge with ¾" brads and a nail set **(photo C).** Place the bottom over the cleats, and secure with ½" brads. When using this method, you'll need to subtract ⅜" from the length and width of the tray bottom when cutting to size.

MAKE THE HANDLES. Transfer the handle pattern onto each

TIP

Routing bits turn clockwise, making the router pull to left. When routing from left to right, place a straightedge fence between the router and you. By placing a straightedge to the left of the router's path, the router will hug the straightedge and naturally help you make better, straighter cuts.

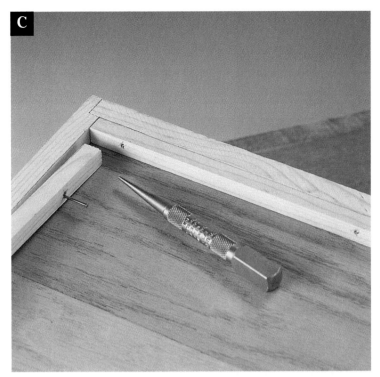

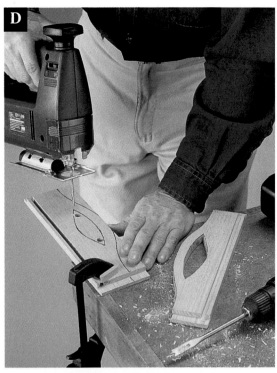

OPTION: *Rather than cut dadoes, you can attach ⅜" stop molding nailed to the tray frame to support the bottom.*

Drill access holes for your jig saw, and carefully cut the handles and curves.

end (see *Diagram*). Drill access holes in the handle and use a jig saw to complete each cut **(photo D).** Sand the cuts smooth.

ASSEMBLE THE TRAY. Cut the tray bottom (C) to size from birch plywood and sand smooth. Test-fit the tray bottom in the grooves of the frame sides and the frame ends. Do not glue the tray bottom in the grooves. Make certain the tray bottom is properly fitted, then apply a thin film of glue to the rabbet joints. To ensure that the glue adheres properly and evenly, use bar clamps to keep the unit tight from end to end and from side to side **(photo E).** Check for square by measuring diagonally from corner to corner. Make any adjustments by slightly realigning the bar clamps until the diagonal measurements are the same. Drill pilot holes through the frame ends into the frame sides,

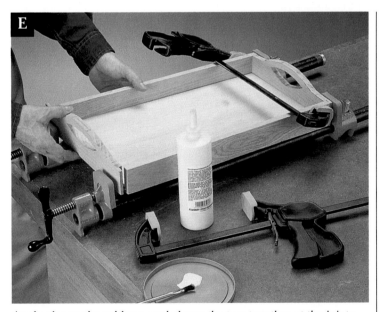

Apply glue to the rabbets, and clamp the tray together at the joints.

and secure the joints with 4d finish nails.

APPLY FINISHING TOUCHES. Scrape off any excess glue at the joints. Finish-sand the tray, wipe off any sanding residue and apply a finish. Mask the bottom, and apply a rustic oak stain on the oak sides and ends.

Then apply a water-resistant topcoat to the sides and ends. A natural oil applied to the birch tray bottom brings out the grain and helps resists moisture from spills.

Gateleg Table

Swing-out tabletop supports transform this wall-hugging oak bistro table into a family-size table.

CONSTRUCTION MATERIALS

Quantity	Lumber
6	1 × 4" × 8' oak
3	1 × 2" × 6' oak
1	¾" × 4 × 8' oak plywood

The fashionable oak gateleg table is a necessity in apartments, cabins and homes where space is tight. Typically, a gateleg table is used as either a modest side table or, when fully extended, as a dinette-style table that seats four. This space-saving design has loftier ambitions. With the end leaves down, the tabletop measures 19 × 48" to provide plenty of space for two diners or for use as a bistro-style serving table. But when the end leaves are raised, this table expands to a spacious 67 × 48", giving you enough space for six diners with full table settings. And all this versatility is offered in a lovely oak package with slat styling in the base.

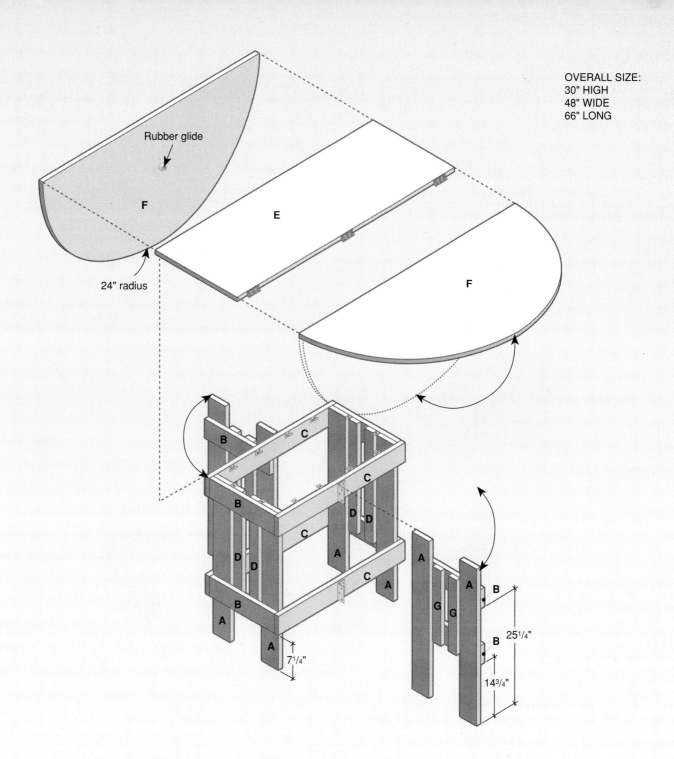

OVERALL SIZE:
30" HIGH
48" WIDE
66" LONG

Rubber glide

24" radius

F

E

F

B

C

C

B

D   D

C

D

A

C   A

A

A

A

A   B

G   G   A

B

B

A

25¼"

7¼"

14¾"

Cutting List				
Key	Part	Dimension	Pcs.	Material
A	Leg	¾ × 3½ × 20¼"	8	Oak
B	Cross rail	¾ × 3½ × 14½"	8	Oak
C	Base rail	¾ × 3½ × 28"	4	Oak
D	Base slat	¾ × 1½ × 21"	4	Oak

Cutting List				
Key	Part	Dimension	Pcs.	Material
F	Table panel	¾ × 19 × 48"	1	Plywood
F	Table leaf	¾ × 24 × 48"	2	Plywood
G	Gate slat	¾ × 1½ × 14"	4	Oak

Materials: Wood glue, brass wood screws (#6 × 1¼", #6 × 2"), 1½ × 3" brass butt hinges (10), oak edge tape (25'), 1¼" brass corner braces (10), ⅞"-dia. rubber bumpers (2), finishing materials.

Note: Measurements reflect the actual thickness of dimensional lumber.

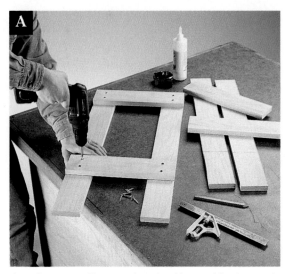

Attach cross rails to each pair of legs with glue and countersunk wood screws.

Position the base slats between the base legs, and attach them to the inside faces of the cross rails.

Directions: Gateleg Table

BUILD THE LEG PAIRS. The support system for the gateleg table consists of four pairs of 1 × 4 legs fastened to short 1 × 4 cross rails. Two of the pairs are connected with base rails to form the main table base, while each swing-out gate sports a single pair of legs.

Start by cutting the legs (A) and cross rails (B) to size. Sand smooth with medium-grit sandpaper to remove any rough cuts. Select four legs and four cross rails to build the main base leg pairs. Lay the legs flat on your worksurface in pairs spaced about 7½" apart. Position a pair of cross rails to span across each leg pair. Arrange the ends of the cross rails flush with the outer edges of the legs, and position the bottom of the lower cross rail 7¼" up from the bottoms of the legs. Keep the upper cross rail flush with the tops of the legs. Attach the cross rails to each leg pair, using wood glue and 1¼" wood screws **(photo A).** Drill pilot holes for the screws, counter-

Sand the table base to smooth out any sharp corners or roughness.

bored for ⅜"-dia. wood plugs. Check with a square to make sure the legs and braces are at right angles to one another before you permanently fasten them together.

Next, assemble the leg pairs for the swing-out gates the same way, except position the bottoms of the cross rails for the gates at 14¾" and 25¼" up from the bottom of the legs.

INSTALL THE SLATS. Each leg pair features two decorative slats attached to the inside

faces of the cross rails.

Cut the base slats (D) and gate slats (G) to length. Turn the base leg pairs over so the cross rails are facedown on your worksurface. Position two base slats on each leg pair so the tops of the slats are flush with the tops of the cross rails and the slats are spaced evenly, with a 1½"-wide gap between slats and the legs. Use pieces of scrap 1 × 2 as spacers. Attach the slats to the cross rails with glue and 1¼" wood screws driv-

Mark the semicircular cutting line for the first table leaf with a bar compass (we made ours from a 25"-long piece of scrap wood).

TIP

Use very fine (400- to 600-grit) synthetic steel wool to buff your project between topcoats. This is especially helpful when using polyurethane, which is quite susceptible to air bubbles, even when very light coats are applied. Be sure to wipe the surface clean before applying the next coat.

en through counterbored pilot holes **(photo B).**

Set the gate slats on the gate cross rails with the same spacing between slats, so the tops and bottoms of the slats are flush with the tops and bottoms of the cross rails. Attach the gate slats with glue and screws.

ASSEMBLE THE TABLE BASE. The table base consists of two pairs of base legs, connected by 1 × 4 side rails.

Cut the base rails (C) to length, then drill a pair of counterbored pilot holes ⅜" in from both ends of each base rail. Prop the leg pairs upright on a flat surface. Apply wood glue to the ends of the base cross rails, then clamp the side rails so the ends are flush with the outer faces of the cross rails and the tops are aligned. Check all the joints for square, then drive 2" wood screws at each joint.

After the glue in the joints has dried, apply glue to ⅜"-dia. wood plugs and insert them into the counterbored screw holes. When this glue has dried,

sand the plugs level. If the plugs protrude more than 1/16", belt-sand with an 80- to 120-grit sanding belt, but take care not to scuff the faces of the rails **(photo C).**

MAKE THE TABLETOP. The tabletop is made from three pieces of plywood, trimmed with oak veneer edge tape. The rectangular table panel is mounted on the table base, and the end leaves are rounded, then attached to the

center panel with butt hinges.

Start by cutting the table panel (E) and table leaves (F) to the full measurements shown in the *Cutting List* on page 93. Use a bar compass to draw a centered, 24"-radius semicircle on one long edge of each leaf. If you don't own a bar compass, create a makeshift one from a 25"-long piece of straight scrap wood. Simply drill a ⅜"-dia. hole with a centerpoint ½" in from one end of the scrap to hold a pencil, then drive a 4d finish nail through a point ½" in from the other end. Attach the finish nail to a piece of plywood butted against one long edge of the leaf, insert the pencil into the hole, and draw the semicircle **(photo D).**

Use an iron to apply oak veneer edge tape to all plywood edges.

Attach the table panel to the base with corner braces.

Attach the leaves to the table panel with 1½ × 3" brass butt hinges.

Carefully cut the semicircle with a jig saw. To even out the cut, clamp a belt sander with a 120-grit belt to your worksurface so the belt is perpendicular to the surface and can spin freely. Lay the table leaf flat on the worksurface (this is very important), and gently press the rounded edge of the leaf up against the sanding belt. Move the board back and forth across the belt until the edges are smooth and there are no irregularities in the semicircle.

Using this table leaf as a template, trace a matching semicircle onto the other leaf. Cut and sand the second table leaf the same way. Finally, apply self-adhesive oak veneer edge tape onto all edges of the table panel and table leaves, using a household iron set at low to medium heat **(photo E).** Trim off any excess tape with a sharp utility knife.

ASSEMBLE THE GATELEG TABLE. Before assembling the table parts, apply wood stain

and a topcoat product (we used water-based polyurethane). After the finish has dried, position the table panel facedown on your worksurface. Center the table base on the underside of the table panel, and attach with 1¼" brass corner braces **(photo F).**

NEXT, BUTT THE TABLE LEAVES against the sides of the table panel, and fasten each leaf panel with two evenly spaced 1½ × 3" brass butt hinges **(photo G).** Attach a butt hinge to the outer face of each base rail, for attaching the gates. Align the hinges so the gate is exactly centered on the rail. Attach a gate to each table side, making sure the tops of the gate and base are flush.

OPEN THE GATES and extend them so they are perpendicular to the table base. Attach a ⅞"-dia. rubber glide to the underside of each leaf as a stop to keep the gate from swinging open too far **(photo H).**

Attach rubber glides to the tabletop to work as stops for the gates.